MW00623628

And Whose Life Are You Living *Anyway?*

What Wise Women Know and Do About Purposeful Living

Angela Kenyatta

And Whose Life Are You Living Anyway?
What Wise Women Know and Do About Purposeful Living

Published by Paradise Valley Press
Chicago, Illinois
www.angelakenyatta.com

Library of Congress Cataloging-in-Publication Data is available.

9 8 7 6 5 4 3 2 1

Cover design by Ian Koviak
Interior design by Domini Dragoone
Printed in the United States of America

DEDICATION

For my beautiful mom,
Electa,
my shero and dearest friend,
with love and gratitude
for being a shining light and
exemplary example of wise womanhood.
You are my eternal inspiration.

Table of Contents

SUITE THREE: REAWAKENING

To our ancestors:
wise women and strong men
who left us rhythm, ritual, and reason
so that we,
across time, ocean, and stolen legacies,
could reclaim selfhood
and find our way back home.

Introduction

Break Me Whole

A heart
once properly broken
sees more clearly
listens more deeply
feels more intensely
and loves more tenderly.
A heart
once properly broken
finds its voice
resurrects itself
reclaims its power
and changes the world.

This is a call to healing.

INTRODUCTION

The Makings of You

You are mighty beyond measure. You're already every bit of the woman you hoped to be. Inside of you lies every ounce of potentiality required to bring the highest intentions for your life into manifestation. Within you is all you've ever needed to become the person you were meant to be. Excellence, brilliance, beauty is your name. If this is both our individual and collective reality as women, why, then, are so many of us lost in the sea of discontent? We're drowning. We're drowning in the noise of a confused world that seeks to shape us into a reality that is not our own. We're caught up in the clamor of other people's expectations, aborted dreams, and self-sabotage. We're trapped amid the clatter of our regrets. We're being ambushed by the busyness of lives that keep us running, seeking, craving, and coveting, yet, in the end, leave us unfulfilled. The insistent bellowing of the world has rendered us deaf to the truth of our own being. *Who would you be without the external pressures you've experienced? What would you do if you knew it didn't have to stay that way? How would you live without the noise?*

The answers await you in the silence of your heart. There you will find the blueprint for building the life you were born to live. There, unencumbered by the outer world, you'll find your talents, gifts, and passions crying out to welcome you—your purpose waiting to lead you home. You are an individualized expression of the Most High. All that you need is within you. This is a call to healing—to heal yourself, to encourage and support others in their healing, and to facilitate the healing of the world. This is the work of wise women.

Invite a group of women into a room and ask them, "What do you want out of life?" Some will immediately pour out their desires, which are brimming from the wellsprings of their hearts. A stream of familiar themes will fill the space: *We want to love and to be loved well. We want greater balance and peace of mind. We want clarity about our reasons for being. We want meaningful work that engages our intellects and honors our contributions. We want to save the world or at least some portion of it.*

Others find it more daunting to connect to the sanctuary within, where the answers to this pivotal question reside. As a result of this spotty connection, their desires for the future are framed as denials rooted in past disappointments. They will tell you that they *don't* want to feel lonely and neglected. They *don't* want to be overworked and underappreciated. They *don't* want to think that this is all there is to living. Even though their vision of tomorrow is only obliquely present, these women are crystal clear that yesterday's more disheartening experiences must be left behind. And then there are those among us who equate fulfillment with material success. You've met this woman; at some point, you may have even been this woman. She can tell you the neighborhood she desires to live in, the car she wants to drive, the salary she aspires to earn, and the projected balances in her IRA and 401K accounts. Yet her picture of life beyond the Louboutin shoes and Hermès handbag remains eerily obscure. She doesn't yet see herself, or her capacity for meaningful contribution, beyond her things. Having "nice things" is not the problem. The challenge arises when material objects are positioned as the foundation upon which identity is formed and sustained. The difficulty for this woman is that the quantity and quality of her "stuff" is how she measures her self-worth.

No matter where we find ourselves along the journey of self-discovery, we are united by the transformational task of getting clear about who we seek to become. Have you asked yourself: *Who will I be five, ten, or thirty years from now? What impact will I have on the world and those around me? What will my legacy be?* Once the future-self vision sharpens, we become more focused on the full expression of the grand design for our lives. How will we ensure that the desire for a purpose-filled life becomes more than a well-lit dream? How will we transcend longing for an inspired life, to actually living one?

Often, we don't receive the answers we seek because we have become overwhelmed by the questions. What is the purpose of life? What does it take to shed the façade and live from the center of one's being? How long will it take to make that happen? Most women are simply too busy going through the motions of life to receive meaningful answers to these questions. Our lives are overwrought with deadlines to meet, projects to finish, and people to please; creating space in our lives for meaningful introspection and disciplined spiritual practice seems an impossible task. Therein sits one of the most significant barriers to real freedom. Many women have a heartfelt desire to live a purposeful life, but they want to reap the spoils without paying the cost of change. The "quick fix, instant mix" aspect of contemporary culture has conditioned far too many of us to buy into the illusion that transforming our lives, like almost everything else, can happen quickly, at a discount and be express-mailed to our doorsteps.

Sometimes we get stuck going through the motions. We buy books, listen to CDs, and attend weekend seminars with a false sense of expectancy, desperately hoping that the *guru du jour* will utter a phrase or a prayer with such transcendent power that we will immediately be reconfigured into a more radiant expression of our most purposeful self. At first, these feel-good fixes satisfy us. We finish the book feeling radically empowered—until the phone rings and the annoyance on the other end of the line disturbs that peace of mind. We leave the seminar basking in bliss until a traffic menace cuts us off and disrupts that euphoric high. We look around after twenty-five years of being Oprah-fied and realize that she's moved on to her next adventure, while an awful lot of the cow manure in our own lives is lookin' pretty much the same. *Houston, we have a problem!*

Such highs are transient by nature because they are built on sand. Just as swiftly as they come, they blow away, knocking us off center and back into the throes of the mediocre existence we so desperately wanted to escape. A purpose-filled life can't be earned vicariously. Nor can it be bequeathed by a benevolent giver. There's no way around the inner transformative work required to redesign your life. It's okay not to have all of the answers up front. You're in good company. No one does. The answers will be revealed as your sense of self, and the expanded vision of your life, unfolds. It is crucial, however, that you fully embrace the questions.

Begin by reviewing the questions that were presented in this section and reflect upon them. As insights come, record them in a personal journal. Write each question on a separate page and include the date at the top. Whenever you receive a new insight pertaining to a particular question, add it to the page along with the new date. Maintaining a journal will facilitate greater self-reflection and encourage the process as you capture important insights.

Not so long ago, during a period in which I was purging and releasing things from my physical environment, I came across a collection of old journals spanning a period of over twenty years. It was fascinating to flip through the pages and be transported back to the people, places, and situations that had inspired my writings. Some passages were exquisitely written and reflected a level of innerstanding that belied my years at the time. As I read, my heart was humbled by the degree of clarity reflected in those earnestly written words. But between you and me, there were other passages that demonstrated a bright-eyed and bushy-tailed naiveté that was rather astonishing. There were mountains of wisdom that I hadn't yet climbed! I couldn't help but laugh at my younger self and give thanks for the grace that freed me from the bondage of my own misunderstandings. In both instances, the retrospective view of my journey reminded me that spiritual evolution is an iterative process, each cycle revealing higher levels of self-knowing, which in actuality is God-knowing. Journaling is a powerful means of documenting your metamorphosis.

How Do We Get There from Here?

The Power of the Universe will come to your assistance if your heart and mind are in Unity.
—NATIVE AMERICAN WISDOM TEACHING

How deep are you willing to go in order to walk in the grace of a purpose-filled life? Almost every woman you know, if asked, can identify something about herself or her situation that she would like to change for the better. Why are the changes that we recognize as the most important to make, often the ones most difficult to manage? The answer lies in understanding the drivers of change and the parameters of their effectiveness.

Information is the most pervasive, yet least potent, driver of change. Information engages the intellect and provides us with data to help drive our decisions. But unless we consciously do something with that information, we can only experience a surface-level encounter with the change we seek. We all know that eating high-quality, nutritionally dense foods and engaging in consistent exercise is a proven pathway to a healthier lifestyle. Yet many of us struggle to incorporate that knowledge into our lives in a manner that results in sustained positive change. If knowing were doing, our communities would be bastions of vibrant health! Information, a surface-level driver, is not enough by itself.

Along the way, as we work to align the outer reality with the inner vision of our lives, we encounter moments of inspiration. We hear an encouraging word or witness someone overcoming an obstacle that we deemed impenetrable in our own lives, and the power of that experience results in a shift in awareness. Whether the inspiration comes through subtle tremor or vociferous quaking, the desire for change transcends the headspace and enters the tabernacle of the heart. One of the first things you'll notice when being driven from the heartspace is the sense of lightness you feel. It's as if some force is breathing new life into you, making even your most heavy-laden affairs seem somehow, if only momentarily, featherweight. Think of a time when you heard a speaker say precisely the thing you needed to hear, at the time you most needed to hear it. The words were so on point that they felt personal. You may have even found yourself thinking, *Who in the world told her* my *business?* Beyond stirring thought, the resonant words penetrated your heart.

When the speech was over, you offered grateful applause, wiped your tear-dappled face, and promptly left your seat to secure a position in the long line of equally inspired devotees who also wanted to get the audio CD. Your intuition was right in guiding you to get that CD, because you soon needed the reminder. Inspiration feels really good, but it is short-lived without reinforcement. The quick hit of inspiration is soon overcome by the long drag of our lives. Inspiration is good, yet we must go deeper still.

Revelation occurs when you transition from material understanding to spiritual knowing. Revelation is the driver that makes the desire to change deeply personal and insatiable. You've heard sacred scriptures recited for years. You've posted verses from your favorite Surahs on sticky notes and carefully placed them around your home. Your back has swayed, and you've waved your hands as the choir sang. You may have even become entranced by the sweet syncopation of your own chanting. Now, something has brought you to the point where what you're hearing and feeling can no longer be experienced as perfunctory participation in religious ritual. You know the power of the Divine because you've seen it realized in your life. The tears that caress your face aren't the result of the extra rehearsal night the choir put in. They are your testimony. Such is the nature of revelation. Sometimes the clarion call of our greater-yet-to-be is so magnetically compelling that we enter this state by our own volition. More often than not, it's our experience of brokenness that bulldozes us into the soul chamber of revelation, the penultimate driver of change.

Transformation is the most highly prized, though often misunderstood, victory for the wise woman sojourner. It is both cause and effect. As we surrender to the prompting of our revelations, we are empowered to envision and enact meaningful and lasting changes in our world of affairs. It is the alpha and the omega. Transformation serves as the launching point, the journey, and the destination of more purposeful living. Change is the one constant with which we all live. You are not the same woman you were yesterday. Each experience in every moment transforms the very nature of who you are. Thus, the goal is to engage the transformation journey mindfully, purposefully, and gracefully. We do so by perpetually cycling through the stages of transformation, continuously emerging as more complete versions of ourselves as each layer of graven identity falls away. Transformation embodies the characteristics of each of the other drivers while simultaneously wedding your knowing and doing. Transformation emblazons and sustains your "do something" nature. You have entered a realm of consciousness where knowing and feeling are no longer sufficient. You are called to act on those things that resonate in your mind and heart. Transformation is the midwife who catches the birth of your emergent womanhood.

THREE STAGES OF TRANSFORMATION: RELEASE, RESTORATION, AND REAWAKENING

Embracing transformation is *grown* woman's work! It commands the courage, commitment, and consistency to lean into what is sometimes a soul-wrenching effort. It requires the audacity to ask hard questions, the wisdom to honor the truth in the answers, and the strength to change course if necessary. It mandates the release of habits of mind and soured emotions not in alignment with the woman you are purposed to become. It calls for letting go of grievances, regrets, and all other emotional shackles that keep you needlessly and painfully bound to your forever-gone past. Are you willing to surrender being right for the sake of walking in righteousness? Are you ready to release blame, judgment, and guilt in order to exercise authority and dominion over the world of your affairs? Are you willing to say goodbye to self-doubt and cast off your fears in order to experience the all-giving, ever-abundant nature of Spirit? Even when burdens are heavy, releasing them can be an arduous task. Yet completing this first step is an essential element of your transformation. Because nature abhors a vacuum, as you release, you must also restore.

The sweetness of restoration calls you to center yourself only in God's truth for your life, forsaking all other notions of what your life can or should be. It necessitates that you fortify your mind with Spirit-inspired thoughts and consistent actions that enrich, empower, and encourage you to stay the course. As you are replenished, you will be reminded of dreams once held close that you might have given up on or that may have slipped beyond your reach. Upon first glance, it may seem that too much time has passed or that too much distance stands between you and the outworking of those dreams. But you look again—this time through the prism of renewed spiritual insight.

You remind yourself that time and space only exist as contingencies in the limited purview of the three-dimensional world. Since you're no longer bound by that world, those parameters have no bearings on your life, and the warmth of once-familiar passions begins to reawaken your soul.

Reawakened, your dreams, talents, gifts, and capabilities are surrendered in service to Spirit. You will be guided to the perfect opportunities to express your purpose. Don't concern yourself with the specifics of how things will unfold. Just stay awake to the guidance you'll receive along the way. As you see the world anew, the divine vision for your life begins to reveal itself with pristine clarity, and you start to excavate the entombed hopes, ambitions, and dreams that have eluded you. The goal is to give new life to your dreams as you offer your unique gifts and talents to the world in service of something greater than yourself. And this time—undergirded by courage, wisdom, and abiding faith in the sovereignty of the Most High in your life—you journey forth with the ease and grace of a gazelle.

The Reflective Essays, Meditative Thoughts, and Wisdom Protocols presented throughout the book are designed to guide you in accomplishing three iterative transformational goals:

1. ***Become more contemplative.*** Thoughtful reflection fosters increased self-awareness, which, over time, leads to greater self-mastery. Through the disciplined practice of contemplation, you will gain meaningful insights into which aspects of your life support the journey towards more purposeful living, and which do not. With increased levels of awareness, you will be better able to chart a course to bring your higher aspirations and goals to fruition.

2. ***Marshal inner wisdom.*** Within you, there are pearls of wisdom as ancient as the sun's first dawning. It's the wisdom of our mothers, our grandmothers, and all of the great mothers before

them. It's the Divine-knowing that sits at the core of our being. "The wisdom from above is first pure, then peaceable, gentle, open to reason, full of mercy and good fruits, impartial and sincere" (James 3:17 NIV). *Yes, please. I'll have some of that.* This is the elevated quality of wisdom that we seek. This is the wisdom that will enable you to answer the questions, "Who must I become in order to fulfill my purpose?" and "How can I best contribute to the world?"

3. ***Live a purpose-filled life.*** Imagine waking up every day knowing exactly why you're alive. Can you picture yourself moving through life with clarity and confidence that your talents and abilities are being used in the most meaningful way? Can you envision a reality in which your day-to-day activities are in full harmony with the values that you hold most dear? This, my sister, is the life that summons you. A purpose-filled life, first and foremost, is an authentic life. Are you eager to design a life that actually supports you in answering the Divine call on your life? Well, congratulations! The journey you're now on is designed to guide you in channeling your inner wisdom to create opportunities for greater self-expression in the world.

As you read the essays, think about how the core ideas relate to your life. As you complete the Wisdom Protocol exercises, cultivate an awareness of where your thoughts travel as you process the experience. Jot down the insights that come to you along the way. Use the Meditative Thoughts to keep you anchored, and strengthen your resolve as you progress. Another feature of this book that you'll notice is the judicious use of questions. While I try to generously share my thoughts and insights, I recognize the importance of facilitating a process that encourages you to think and reflect more deeply on your own life. After all, this book is designed to support you in attaining a more purpose-filled life! As you proceed through the text, you'll be encouraged to move beyond a surface-level interaction with the ideas being presented. A plethora of benefits accompanies whole-hearted engagement with meaningful questions, including increased critical thinking, a more thorough analysis of ideas, discoveries, and better decision-making. If you come across questions that are difficult to answer, simply make note of them and continue on your journey of self-exploration. This will allow you to look back at them, over time, to discern any themes or commonalities that emerge. Making connections between the places where you get stuck can lead to very compelling insights. Pay attention to the themes that emerge. They are important keys to unlocking the mystery of self-mastery!

WHAT'S YOUR LIFE TELLING YOU?

There are usually signs. Rarely do we awaken to sudden and inexplicable discontent. Most of the time, the telltale signs are there all along, but we're either too busy to notice or we've reinterpreted the data to better reflect what we want to see and hear. For example: "Well, he didn't actually propose, but he was talking about the future and he mentioned me. That's why I thought we'd be together forever." Yet, despite our proclivity for sometimes distancing ourselves from common sense, our lives continue to whisper, speak, and—if necessary—blast the truth of our experiences. Think about your life. What's bringing you the greatest joy? What's causing you the deepest pain? In which areas have you found the most contentment? Where is the peace that you seek "a day late and a dollar short"? Think about your state of mind. Is your life okay or pretty good, or are you living life's best? Be careful not to judge the message: Just listen to what your life is telling you about where you are at this moment. The sooner you hear and heed what life is telling you, the better able you will be to successfully navigate the course.

Years ago, I experienced a recurring dream in which I was joyously pregnant and awaiting the birth of a baby. Drifting into the dream was mellow and sweet, but not for long. Sadly, it always ended the same way—I would experience a spontaneous abortion, a miscarriage. Joy and anticipation were replaced by a profound sense of loss and disappointment. Curled up in agony on the hospital bed, I'd try with all of my might to hold the baby inside of me. But despite my best efforts, my body would yield to the contractions, and the not-yet-ready-to-be-born baby would pass from my womb. Rivers would form from my tears. At this point, in each dream, a radiant, warm-hearted, and resolute woman would enter the room to comfort me. Lovingly and with calm assurance, she would speak to me: "It's okay, honey. Just breathe. There'll be another chance. No worries: It'll happen for you. Just trust. There's nothing to fear." Although I couldn't see her face clearly through the well of my tears, I was comforted by her presence.

For the longest time, I struggled to understand the persistence and significance of the dream, so I prayed and asked for insight. For several months after making my prayerful inquiry, the dream eluded me, and I didn't miss it, honestly. Finally, the dream returned, this time in much greater detail, and my life was changed forever. In this version, I was in the same birthing room, in the same bed, but this time I was ecstatic with joy as I held my healthy new baby for the first time. Then one of those peculiar dream-state phenomena happened. Beaming with bliss, I looked my newborn in the face and saw myself. It wasn't a baby that looked like me; it was literally me. I'd given birth to myself. I clearly recognized myself as both mother and child. Stay with me, because it gets better.

Once again, the beautifully radiant woman appeared. This time she didn't speak. Instead, she sat gently at my bedside as she held my hand and lovingly smiled at us. My heart overflowed with gratitude to her for consistently being there to coach, counsel, and comfort me. She had been the clear and confident presence that walked with me through the valleys of doubt, fear, and disappointment. I was elated that she was also present to share in my joy. I looked up at her to express my thanks and, to my surprise, saw yet another incarnation of myself. But she wasn't the person that I was at that moment. She was more physically and spiritually mature—a more fully expressed realization of the young woman I was at that time. She was the woman I could one day become.

To tell the truth, when I first woke up I didn't know what to think. Had I watched *A Christmas Carol* one time too many? Carefully, I recorded the details of the dream in my journal and prayed for understanding. Over the next few days, the mysteries of the dreams revealed themselves to me. There were several key messages: Spirit had already equipped me with everything needed to give birth to the grandest and fullest expression of my life, but those gifts, talents, and abilities had to be correctly nurtured within me before taking form in the world. There were aspects of my life that were not providing optimal nourishment for my development, and if I didn't address them, I would risk aborting the chance to live my most purposeful life. I would have to take responsibility for showing up for myself and nurturing that life and that woman into being. The spirit of God within had come to me, through me, and as me—in the form of a dream—to speak to the deepest yearnings of my heart and to assure me that I wasn't on the journey alone. That was the last time I ever had that dream. Knowing that the Universal Life Force has got your back strengthens and encourages you. So, with wide-open eyes, I began to examine my life.

A PRETTY GOOD LIFE

My life at the time wasn't a bad life at all. In fact, it was pretty good! It was safe, respectable, and *really* predictable. I was in my twenties, recently divorced, and the mother of the most amazing little boy. Even though the marriage had ended, I had strong, loving support from my parents as I raised my son. My life was rich with extended family and friends, and I was reasonably happy. Dutifully, I reported to work and did a "good job" satisfying the responsibilities of my "good job," even though I craved greater creative and intellectual fulfillment. Romantically, I was in a relationship that wasn't a bad relationship, with a man who wasn't a bad man. He just wasn't the man for me, even though he was a solid companion and a good friend with whom I'm glad to have shared part of my life. My social life was active and fun, but uninspired. I was a social butterfly with a short wingspan. Spiritually, I was an earnest seeker who was frustrated about not finding answers to the questions that captivated me the most about my life's purpose and how to fully express it.

There are many other examples, but I suspect that you've already gotten the point. I'd settled into the "security" of the life in front of me. In many ways, it was the safety and respectability of that life that made it inherently more dangerous. Being too comfortable and feeling too safe are among the biggest impediments to living a purposeful life. When there's nothing to lose and nothing to give up, either because you've never had it or because you've lost it all, there's often a greater willingness to take risks. But when there are "just enough" creature comforts to keep the carrot of contentment dangling out front, we are quickly seduced into maintaining the status quo—often at the expense of losing our authentic selves. That's precisely where I was at that moment in my life. Over time, if we fail to act, we become like spinning tires in thick mud, and we get stuck.

What about you? Have you ever been in a similar situation? You're living a "pretty good" life. According to external standards, you've "done something with yourself." And depending on where you started, you may have already exceeded the early expectations of what your life would become. Others may look toward you in admiration. There may be people around you living very similar lives who wonder how it's even possible that you could desire something different, because they've found fulfillment from a place you seek to escape. Some will be well aware of how you feel because they share in your discontent. A few of those will just want to keep you around for company anyway!

Yet despite the opinions of others, the emptiness you feel threatens to swallow you whole. You spend your days being what everyone else thinks you should be, and then you lie awake at night wondering how to fill the hollowness inside. Sometimes you actually feel guilty for your discontent. At other times, you try to ignore it. In the meantime, your soul continues to cry out, but you're not sure how to answer. With all certainty, however, you know that something has to give. It doesn't matter how satisfying your life may seem to the external world. No matter how much the world celebrates who you are, if who you are and what you are doing don't resonate with your spirit, you owe it to yourself to find out why.

As you complete the "Life Inventory" exercise, remember that there are no right or wrong answers. Be completely candid with yourself. This is an opportunity to take an honest inventory of your life in order to better navigate the journey of transformation you are now undertaking.

LIFE INVENTORY EXERCISE

Spend some quality time reflecting on the following questions, and record your responses in your personal journal. To go even deeper, identify a partner with whom you can discuss the exercise by taking turns sharing the questions and answers.

1. How happy are you with the life you're currently living?
2. Which aspects of your life bring you the greatest joy?
3. Which aspects of your life are the most significant sources of discontentment?
4. Is there a gap between the woman you are today and the woman you'd like to become? If so, in which areas of your life do you most feel the disconnection?
5. How strong is your current support network? Who's on your go-to list for wisdom and support?
6. Name three things you would most like to change about your personal life.
7. Name three things you would most like to see different in the world.

SUITE ONE

Release

Sometimes you've got to let everything go—purge yourself. If you are unhappy with anything, whatever is bringing you down, get rid of it. Because you'll find that when you're free, your true creativity, your true self comes out.

—TINA TURNER

The Sweetness of Release

Each change, whether welcomed or uninvited,
radical or discreet,
moves us that much closer to
the realization of the emerging self.
Knowing that this is true,
we hold fast to the promise of even more radiant tomorrows
and lovingly release all indigent thoughts,
useless habits,
decrepit conditions,
barren relationships,
and any other worn-out thing,
that would hinder this grand becoming.
And so it is.
Ashe'.
Ameen.
Selah.

CHAPTER 1

Slave Hearts, Serpent Tongues, and Soul Wounds

In the Dagara tradition,
where the wound lays the gift also lives.
—SOBONFU SOMÉ

Before we explore the sweet freedom of release, let's examine the internal and external obstacles that keep us bound. At some point, we've all experienced hurt and humiliation. Maybe you were the subject of a gossip's tongue or on the receiving end of an angry rant. Perhaps you were violated physically, emotionally, or both. Sometimes it's the sting of a false accusation that renders you numb for years. Or the stench of betrayal that leaves you wondering if you'll ever be able to trust again. We've all been there. Whether bruised by another's callousness or shattered by the cruelty we sometimes inflict upon ourselves, we each bear our own crosses.

Just as we've had to shore ourselves up and put our broken pieces back together following painful encounters with others, somewhere in time we've also left some folks licking wounds. Unintentionally, or from a state of ill-conceived deliberateness, at some point all of us have failed to bring the best of who we are to the people and situations that shape our lives. Hurting each other remains an unperfected part of the human experience. What happens when acidic words have been hurled and can't be taken back? What happens after an unthinkable act has crash-landed into the center of your reality? How do you move on? Most of us have mastered letting minor offenses roll off our shoulders. But how do we handle the experiences that have had a more significant impact? How do we reconcile the righteous desire for justice with the divine necessity of grace? If love is both the quintessential pathway and the ultimate destination, how do we find our way there when reality is sent spiraling out of control in its seeming absence?

An enslaved heart remains captive to painful memories from the forever-gone past. The recurring memories reign supreme, like a despotic master intent on never allowing your consciousness to venture far from the experiences you'd most like to leave behind. Years, even decades may have passed, but when your heart is enslaved, you remain emotionally blocked and bound in the chamber of your haunted thoughts and emotions. Whenever our hearts are in bondage, our tongues are also defiled, which hinders our ability to create in a manner reflective of the divine presence within. We can't effectually speak joy, peace of mind, and the fulfillment of purpose into existence as long as our hearts harbor feelings of anger, unrighteousness, unworthiness, or unforgiveness. To speak, of course, is more than the vocalization of thought; it includes the deeply held intention behind what is spoken. The serpent tongue is venomous because it attacks the belief that something better is possible, necessary, and deserved. The serpent tongue shows up in many ways. Sometimes the words of another can dampen enthusiasm or weaken our resolve. At other times, we may carelessly allow the unruliness of our own tongues to wreak havoc in someone else's life. But most often, the serpent tongue spreads its poison internally, rendering the conversations that we have within ourselves the most damning and damaging. How many times have you talked yourself out of pursuing a dream?

We live in the land of the walking wounded. To one degree or another, we've all sustained wounds from the human experience. These wounds exist on many planes: emotional, spiritual, physical, and even psychological. They vary in intensity. Some are deeply rooted, while others rest on the surface. The scars of some wounds are easily seen, while others become apparent only when we bump into them. Some heal neatly, leaving little evidence that something harmful has happened. Others linger for what seems like eternity, remaining violently gaping and intensely painful. We all carry wounds of some sort. Most of these injuries heal with time and proper care, and we are able to find our way back to wholeness. But some wounds have a different nature. Soul wounds languish in seas of such severity that their healing requires expert and protracted care.

A soul wound is indicative of a severe breach in the foundation of one's emotional and moral nature. A soul wound occurs when lower-level expressions of human nature override the expression of one's divinity. It is a clear sign of deep and enduring emotional and/or psychological distress. Soul wounds often manifest as character disorders typified by thoughts, feelings, words, and behaviors being governed by pain instead of discernment, heart, or reason. The pervasive lack of insight and diminished self-restraint result in a compromised moral compass and accompanying aberrant behaviors. Soul wounds are the cumulative effect of traumas that have gone unhealed. The impacts of soul wounds are all around us. How often do you hear about some abhorrent and unethical act being inflicted upon someone in your city or community?

The probability is high that at some point you will cross paths with someone who is gravely wounded in this way. Many intelligent, highly functional, hardworking people harbor deep emotional and psychological wounds. Some of them are in positions of authority. Barely a week goes by in which the fall of some upstanding citizen isn't chronicled publicly. And, almost always, there's a loved one, neighbor, colleague, or congregant who just can't fathom that the person they know is capable of the moral breaches and atrocities they're accused of committing. But even casual research into the prevalence of character disorders, and similarly clustered personality disorders informs us that we shouldn't be surprised at all.

If we conceptualize soul wounds as existing along a broad spectrum of severity, the perpetration of evil—the destructive use of the mind—can be understood as the most extreme and debased form of expression. Philosophers, theologians, and clinicians debate about the origins of evil and whether its roots are moral, spiritual, or psychological. For the purposes of our discussion we'll use as our working definition the one posed by philosopher A.K. Fayemi, who, through the lens of African cosmology, defines evil as "deliberately acting with the intention to destroy, discredit or obstruct the achievement of goals, ideas, happiness or general well-being" of another. Or, in other words, the essence of evil is the intentional harm of another. Perpetrators of evil understand the difference between right and wrong but have turned away from God and their own humanity. In Western psychology, clinicians often cite *malignant narcissism*—the most severe pathology, characterized by "extreme, exploitative selfishness"—as the psychological root cause of the most vicious acts of inhumanity. Psychiatrist and author M. Scott Peck defines evil as "the exercise of political power—that is the imposition of one's will upon others by overt or covert coercion—in order to avoid extending one's self for the purpose of nurturing spiritual growth. Peck continues:

> *There really are people and institutions made up of people, who respond with hatred in the presence of goodness and would destroy the good insofar as it is in their power to do so. They do*

> *this not with conscious malice but blindly, lacking awareness of their own evil—indeed, seeking to avoid any such awareness. As has been described of the devil in religious literature, they hate the light and instinctively will do anything to avoid it, including attempting to extinguish it. They will destroy the light in their own children and in all other beings subject to their power. Evil people hate the light because it reveals themselves to themselves.*

Soul wounds are expressed through human consciousness—the sum total of the beliefs, emotions, ideas, and thoughts held in mind that shape character and drive behavior. That's the meaning behind the often-quoted saying, "Consciousness really is *everything.*" Love is the highest expression of consciousness and evil is the lowest expression of consciousness.

Soul wounds afflict the collective consciousness, just as they exist within the consciousness of an individual. We need only to look around the world at the persistent patterns of conflict that plague many nations to see that this is true. Unhealed wounds, many of which have festered across generations, cry out for proper care. Nowhere is this any more evident than here in the United States, where soul wounds, rooted in her original sin of racism, continue to stifle the realization of her full potential. The ideology of white supremacy sits at the core and has shaped the formation of every American institution. The dispensation of unjust punishment and unearned privilege based on race, which was initiated at the very formation of this country, remains prevalent and toxic. The ideology of white supremacy is like bad air in a big city. Despite continually inhaling and exhaling it, most inhabitants don't question the quality or the effects of the bad air. They just keep breathing.

America's insidious nature of racism can be difficult to recognize, primarily by those who are too blinded by privilege to see what's being hidden in plain sight. The policies, practices, and norms of structural racism function much like the operating system of a computer; it runs quietly in the background driving performance, as coded, to maintain the status quo. Unless there's a glitch, it's easy to forget that the operating system is even there. Yet it's ever-present, managing every activity of the hardware and software on the computer. We discover similar dynamics when we explore the perpetuation of sexism, classism, religious intolerance, and other social constructs that are as real as the people who are subjected to their tyranny.

Soul wounds exist on many levels. Individual, familial, community, national, and global. Denying the existence of soul wounds doesn't make them go away. Ignoring soul wounds doesn't mitigate their impact. Placing a bandage on soul wounds doesn't heal them. Soul wounds demand thoughtful care by mindful and skillful caregivers. That's why we're here: to contribute in some way to healing the world. Our call is not to look away from what pains us, but to cast our sight beyond current conditions and catch hold of the divine vision seeking to be brought to fruition. Creating heaven on earth can only happen through us.

We've all heard the old adage—"Hurt people hurt people"—and pained people are all around us. How, then, do we heal our own wounds and buffer ourselves from the afflictions of others? Self-care is essential to personal well-being and the restoration of our families and communities. When we are standing on solid ground spiritually, emotionally, mentally, and physically, we are better able to navigate the terrains of life, no matter what comes. When we show up as wise and responsible women who mindfully tend our own emotional and psychological gardens, we are more capable of supporting the healing of others and establishing healthy boundaries that buffer us from harm.

WISE WOMEN AND HEALERS

Wise women are called to heal and to be healers. The divine plan for us is that we be made whole in every area of our lives. But a sacred *yes* is required before the healing can take place. This means saying *yes* to your own healing and answering the call to become a healing force in the world. One of the most effective ways to activate the sacred *yes* is to immerse yourself in the process of release. By setting free the attitudes, feelings, habits, and relationships that no longer serve your emergent being, you create space on the landscape of your consciousness for restoration and the reawakening of your divine nature. The Reflective Essays, Meditative Thoughts, and Wisdom Protocols in this section are designed to support you in relinquishing everything that obscures your clear vision of yourself and the life you are purposed to live. Learning to let go is the initiation into the sisterhood of wise womanhood.

CHAPTER 2

Learning to Let Go

If you surrendered to the air, you could ride it.

—TONI MORRISON

Once we realize that an idea, habit, situation, or relationship has run its course, we can begin to contemplate how to release it from our lives. Even when we know that letting go is the right thing to do, the process is complicated. The biggest obstacle is often our resistance to liberating ourselves from the source of familiar discontent. For some, a known pain is more comfortable to bear than an uncertain future without it. This is why so many of us linger in a barren land long after it has stopped producing fruit. How many people do you know who've languished in some manner of deep discontent in perpetuity? Learning to let go is a prerequisite to moving forward. Some exits are elegant, graceful, and relatively uneventful. We muster up the inner resolve to act decisively and make it so!

Yet there are other times when the intense vibration of the departure causes glass to shatter and valuables to crash to the floor as you metaphorically slam the door behind you. Letting go has many timbres, and you must discover which one works for your particular situation. Whether you're giving up gossip, releasing a long-held grievance, or bidding adieu to an unhealthy relationship, letting go begins with the decision to trust that the magnificence seeking to emerge through you is worth the work required to set yourself free from encumbrances.

There are times when letting go is no longer a choice but a necessity. Some bitter root has taken hold of you and shows no signs of loosening its grip. What do you do in situations that test the limits of your capacity to love and forgive? Does letting go mean giving up or giving in? Absolutely not. To release is to choose life, to summon grace, and to pursue healing. Sometimes the process of letting go requires that you cut straight to the core, to release false notions of self that hinder development. That's the lesson that Ashley, a peace activist and artist, who works in higher education, learned once she began to really see herself clearly.

"Growing up, I was socialized and developed into the stereotypical 'Strong Black Woman,'" Ashley explains. "I was content with being the Black woman that *everyone* could rely on. As I got older, I built my identity around serving others. And it was okay, because as a Black woman, I needed someone to see me, even if it was as the 'helper.' After all, who was *I* without *them*?" If we could each collect a single dollar for every mother, daughter, sister, niece, cousin, and sistah-friend who has experienced not being seen while in plain sight, we'd all be rich! This is among the most common ways that women, especially women of color (WOC), are denied power. It's a silent form of subjugation that wears really, really thin. Ashley certainly isn't the first or last among us to adopt the Superwoman persona as a means of seeking visibility and thereby acquiring validation of her humanity and worth. Oh, the roads we travel . . .

Ashely continues: "It became clear that people valued my *labor*, my *ideas*, my *genius*—but they did not value *me*. Over time, I became fed up with being Superwoman. It no longer served me, and I made a conscious decision to let go of this identity." Do you remember where you were and what the circumstances were when you, like Ashley, finally said to yourself, "I just can't do this anymore. I simply *will not* do this any longer"? Something spectacular happens when we stand in the awareness of the relationship between our conditions and our inner beliefs: We become keenly aware of our power to effect change. Ashley recognized the inextricable link between the identity she'd embraced and the way she was being treated by others. She moved beyond the stereotype of the Strong Black Woman and the prevailing social conditioning that continue to give it life. She skipped right over the power dynamics that fuel the assignment of invisibility as a means of diminishing women, and she confronted her undesirable conditions in the arena where she possessed the greatest power: her own mind. Once the lightbulb went on, Ashley got it! Whatever is created in mind can be changed in mind. The instant that Ashley made the conscious decision to lay down the Superwoman identity, it no longer held any sway over her life.

Once a true knowledge of self sinks in, we realize that we are capable of rocking entire worlds out of their orbit. Aha! Did you feel a surge of energy shooting through your body upon merely entertaining the thought of possessing that kind of power? That's who we are, Sis. Sometimes we spend a disproportionate amount of time focusing on the outer world, when mastery of our inner reality is the true pathway to freedom. Correcting a single errant thought can cause a seismic shift in your conditions. Ashley breaks it down like this: "Upon my abrupt retreat, slowly, surely, I became visible to everyone. It baffled me—how I could *disappear* and folks could suddenly see me." Now, that's deep, isn't it? Once she began to truly see herself, the world could no longer deny her presence. Just let that sink in for a moment. Powerful, isn't it?

Ashley didn't find the letting-go process difficult at all. Once she became clear within herself about who she was, releasing those who had neither valued nor humanized her didn't pose a challenge. Good-bye. Once her inner vision was clear, her outer actions lined up accordingly. Ashley was free of the compulsion to prove her value by overextending herself to others. But her work still wasn't done. Seldom does the act of letting go mark the end of the process. Often there are interior wounds left behind that require our loving care—the residual scars that come from having lingered too long in desolate places. Ashley wrestled with the anger and guilt that haunted her, saying, "The difficulty was in learning to value my life, and to forgive myself for having neglected *me* for so long. Once I let go of the anger that I felt toward others for not humanizing me, and the guilt that I felt for not humanizing myself, I was liberated." Dear Sistah, will you, too, be set free?

You are bound to lose some people and some things as you find yourself. Proclaim it all good. And, surely, as your emergent self rises into being, aspects of your former self will fall away. Do not resist the process. This, too, is as it should be. Ashley puts in all in perspective: "One thing that I have learned about the value of being able to let go is that while it is a strange process—and sometimes painful—in the long run, you will not regret it."

The first order of business is to identify, explore, and let go of every internal and external constraint that hinders the full expression of your divine purpose. The guides on the following pages will support you as you undertake this part of your transformation journey. If you're taking this on as a solo project, simply repeat the Wisdom Protocols as often as needed until you feel the freedom of release being activated within you. This may mean spending several days addressing one aspect of release and only a few hours working with another. Divesting more challenging strongholds will require significantly more time and energy, and that's perfectly okay. Your process must be guided by your unique needs. If you're working with a partner or a group, the same approach applies, only now you'll be sharing your insights and experiences with others. Remember to keep writing your journal notes in either instance. One of the most rewarding experiences will be to look back on your notes at some point in the future and celebrate the progress you've made.

MEDITATIVE THOUGHT

I lovingly release any thought, behavior, condition, or relationship that hinders the expression of my higher self.

WISDOM PROTOCOL

Have a conversation with someone you trust about what you'd like to accomplish as you focus on releasing nonproductive thoughts, feelings, behaviors, or experiences from your life. This protocol is designed to support you in two ways: First, it provides an opportunity to take inventory of which of your current relationships have the foundation of trust needed to support you on your transformation journey. Second, it invites you to practice a degree of vulnerability, which creates the space for greater intimacy in relationships. Of course, if this isn't the right time to partner in the completion of this protocol, journal your responses instead. You know what's best. But when you're done, read what you've written aloud. There is power in hearing and feeling the vibration of your truth.

CHAPTER 3

And Who Do They Say That I Am?

You can't have relationships with other people until you give birth to yourself.

—SONIA SANCHEZ

It's not uncommon to meet women who have been tremendously unhappy in some aspects of their lives for many years, but stayed because of the pay, prestige, stability, or familiarity the situation provided. Many have remained despite the high costs of diminished self-esteem, compromised relationships, and/or being totally out of alignment with the work they feel purposed to do. There's a reason why people remain in the barren lands of their lives. The external world is masterful at convincing us that it's the source of our good; and as long as we are subject to that programming, we look outside of ourselves for sustenance. The deeper the conditioning, the more dependent we become on external definition and validation. Over time, we come to rely on the vestiges of that world to remind us of who we are. If you were to ask people "Who are you?" and they were to answer without filters, many of the responses would be unsettling.

"I am my job title."
"I am a vanishing appendage to my husband."
"I am my social circle."
"I am my ZIP code."
"I am the personification of my family's fears."
"I am my mistakes and what you think about them."
"I am my social, political, or religious cause."
"I am the expectations of my parents."
"I am the name I was called last night."
"I am whoever you say that I am."

Whenever a woman derives her sense of self from anyone or anything outside of herself, she becomes subject to an external master. Her well-being inextricably linked to what that master says she can do and be. Giving birth to oneself can be difficult when constantly under the barrage of externally imposed identities and expectations. Yet this is precisely the soul-liberating work we are called to do. That's why this journey is about waking up and claiming dominion over your life! We give birth to ourselves by beginning with an honest examination of our lives. We explore where we feel most whole and where we are in the greatest need of healing. Through this process of self-discovery, we begin to better understand where our most profound, most authentic truth lives and where its absence denies us power. In deciding to give birth to ourselves, we heal our lives and grant ourselves permission to fully unleash the gifts, talents, and possibilities seeking expression through us.

The ability to define oneself is essential to our humanity. It's a right that we must hold especially dear as women of color, whose social identities have been steeped in stereotypes fueled by racism, misogyny, and other forms of psychosocial violence. We are called to look beyond the socially constructed inventions of Sapphire, super-nannies, and overly sexualized video vixens to a truth that can neither be forsaken nor denied. The most powerful driving force behind all that we will ever do or become is how we define ourselves, and the manner in which we see ourselves in relationship to the world. Regardless of what anyone else says, it's what *we believe* about ourselves that matters most. This is our inward and ever-enduring truth.

Until we awaken to our divine nature, existent beyond all humanly manufactured notions of self, our reality will remain skewed. We will continue to remake ourselves in the image and likeness of the world. And as long as we treat the world as if it's our source, we will sacrifice ourselves to its demands. Acknowledging Spirit—alone—as our infinite source grounds us and gives us the steady footing needed to successfully navigate life.

Right now, at this very moment, vow to emancipate yourself from the attachment to false identities. Let them go! Ahhh, see how good that feels? It's like stepping out from in front of the funhouse mirror and seeing a clear reflection of yourself for the very first time! In the end, here's the only question that really matters, *Who do you say that you are?*

MEDITATIVE THOUGHT

I am brilliant, beautiful, and beloved just as I am.
I release any attachments to false identities and
courageously give birth to my most authentic self.

WISDOM PROTOCOL

Make a list of ten "I am" statements that describe how you see yourself. Be as courageous and honest as possible. Then, review the list and identify any statements that you would like to change. With a partner or in your journal, explore why you desire to release those statements and the energy that they carry. Rewrite each of them to reflect the attributes you would like to give birth to in that area of your life.

CHAPTER 4

Living on Borrowed Thoughts

To identify the enemy is to free the mind.

—MARI EVANS

Whose idea of life are you currently living? Pop culture programming consistently seeks to inculcate us with random and pernicious definitions of what it means to be genuinely alive. Over time, if we aren't careful, our thoughts become infused with whatever ideas the environment happens to offer up at the moment. "Like this." "Don't like that." "Your butt is too big!" "Your house is too small." "*This* will make you happy, but *that* never will." External forces seek to dictate, or at least influence, everything—from which career we pursue to whom we love. The messages are communicated to us through media and music, within our communities, at the workplace, in our places of worship, and often by the people closest to us—many of whom are unknowingly trapped inside their own externally contrived realities.

Whenever your mind is surrendered to what the external world says about you and your life, the longing to evolve remains unsatisfied. Instead of seeking and surrendering to the highest vision for your life, you set yourself up for a brutally exhausting, and ultimately futile, game of cat and mouse. Each awkward step places you in rapid pursuit of a strange and moving target: the unattainable ideal. Have you noticed how quickly some people surrender their minds to the ideas of others? Seemingly, they sway with whatever flow of ideas enters their lives, moving whichever way the winds of the collective consciousness happen to blow. For example, you'll hear people professing a virulent hatred for people in another part of the world even though they've never been to that place or met any of those people personally. Somewhere along the way, someone parented that thought for them and passed it on. They simply accepted the idea and transitioned from being a passive recipient to an active perpetrator.

When your mind is subject to external rule, critical thinking isn't required or desired. This is why some people routinely vote against public policies that are in their best interest while supporting others that contribute to their demise. It's why some seek solace in "alternative facts." When you're tacitly committed to groupthink, it's easier—and often preferable—to blindly accept a lie than to wrestle with the truth. Wisdom cautions that if you care enough to have an opinion, you must also care enough to weigh the facts; but many turn a deaf ear to her advice.

Look around you. Often the borrowed thoughts that pose the greatest threat to a healthy sense of selfhood are those supplanted in the more intimate spaces that we share with others: our homes, communities, places of worship, and social groups. We get caught up in trying too hard to fit in. We risk losing ourselves by living into other people's visions. If we are not mindful, we will find ourselves morphing, bending, and stretching unnaturally in an attempt to fit into forms imposed by others. Shape-shifting into personae that are unrecognizable to the authentic self. This is both an individual and collective challenge. Sometimes entire communities of people find themselves ensnared by borrowed thoughts, as Maysun's story illustrates.

MAYSUN'S GIFT

Among the gifts that Maysun received for her sixteenth birthday was a box of cosmetic products from her aunt, Fran, who was visiting for the summer from Nigeria. The box included nail polish, lip gloss, perfume, shampoo, and a jar of beauty cream. Maysun's aunt explained that it was of the utmost importance, now that Maysun was approaching womanhood, for her to take good care of herself. Finally, Maysun had an adult ally who didn't think she was too young to begin experimenting with cosmetics. With the blessing of her parents, Maysun excitedly started using the products. She enjoyed the sweet scent of her fragrance wafting through the air as she walked to school with her friends. The pop of subtle color on her lips and the rainbow that adorned her nails were also sources of personal satisfaction. But before long, the beauty cream that Maysun had been using caused her face to become irritated. She told her aunt what was happening, but her aunt encouraged her to continue using the cream anyway, explaining that her skin would soon get used to it. But it didn't. The itchiness and inflammation only worsened.

Maysun shared her concerns with her mother, who immediately suggested they go to the computer to look up the ingredients listed on the beauty cream's container: Hydroquinone, mulberry, aloesin, lemon extract, and other agents. It turned out that the beauty cream was actually a bleaching product designed to depigment the skin. Maysun's mother, Chinyere, was furious. Aunt Fran had managed to bring a bootlegged skin whitener, along with the corresponding colonial mentality, all the way from Africa to England, to be passed on to Maysun. When confronted, Aunt Fran wasn't shy about saying she had acted in the best interest of her niece: "Maysun, she's a pretty girl. But she's as dark as the night! And she's going to be single all the days of her life if she stays that way."

Well, Aunt Fran was right on one account. Maysun was a mocha-colored wonder. She looked as if the melanin gods had kissed her from head to toe, anointing her body with deep, lush tones indicative of her African ancestry. But Aunt Fran was wrong about the rest. Like far too many darkly pigmented women *and men* around the world, she had been indoctrinated to believe that the European standard of beauty was superior to all others. Fairer skin, under this neocolonial mindset, was aspirational, even at the cost of chronic illness or death.

The internalization of this self-effacing borrowed thought is still driving the behaviors of millions of people today. False ideas, equally as ridiculous as this one, are insidiously propagated through popular culture more than we acknowledge. This is why we must critically analyze the thoughts and beliefs that we hold dear and be willing to unpack them so that their origins can be understood.

The grossly misguided thinking about what constitutes beauty is so pervasive that the sale of skin-lightening products has grown into a multibillion-dollar industry, as Black, Brown, and Yellow people across the globe attempt to alter their appearance and adhere to standards that were externally imposed upon them. This mass self-flagellation is the outgrowth of generations of psychological trauma that, for some, has resulted in the internalization of the belief that whiteness is inherently better and more beautiful. The use of bleaching products has been banned in several African countries due to continued widespread use despite the known health risks.

Fortunately for Maysun, her parents were intelligent, thoughtful, critical thinkers who were well aware of the impact that these types of extraneous messages could have on their children. Rather than borrowing thoughts from the popular culture, or passively allowing them to infiltrate their home, Chinyere and Oba proactively parented in ways that affirmed a sense of healthy selfhood in their children. Their home was filled with images that celebrated African people and culture. Television viewing was a weekend-only activity. And even then, the parents carefully curated what their children could view. They encouraged intellectual curiosity and rewarded it with rich experiences, including museum visits, harvest days at a local farm, and live theater performances. They openly challenged ideas that sought to distort or subjugate Black interests. They modeled critical thinking, teaching their children to question the world around them and to form their own opinions. Chinyere and Oba understood that raising emotionally healthy, self-confident, and intellectually astute children required active engagement and intentional action. They were cognizant of the fact that when children grow up in homes where they are affirmed and supported, they are less vulnerable to the influence of outside forces.

The beauty cream incident became a teaching moment for Maysun's family. They used this as an opportunity to engage Aunt Fran and others in critical conversations about the damaging impact of holding on to beliefs that fundamentally and assiduously disaffirm people of color. They also vigorously debunked the idea that being acceptable to a man should be the criteria by which their daughter should make decisions about how she presents herself to the world. As for Maysun, she took it all in stride. She tossed the cream, took an up-close selfie of her gorgeous chocolate face, and posted it on Facebook—along with the hashtags #MyBlackIsBeautiful and #BlackGirlMagic.

Despite being exposed to the same external stimuli, critical thinkers are much more deliberate about what they allow to take residence in their consciousness. These beings evaluate thoughts and ideas against the truth of their inner compass and allow divine wisdom to guide their actions. In a "groupthink" world, the free thinker is often misunderstood because of her penchant for going against the grain. She won't hate upon suggestion or love on demand. She's not interested in becoming another Madison Avenue makeover. She's fully committed to the full expression of her authentic self and unleashing her unique gifts and talents into the world. What about you? Who is your mental master? What's the state of your mind—bound or free?

MEDITATIVE THOUGHT

I am a critical thinker and my mind is free.

WISDOM PROTOCOL

Identify one thought or belief you hold that makes you somewhat uncomfortable, and then answer the following questions about that thought:

1. What's the origin of the thought? (Think about when you first became aware that you held the thought. Where were you? What were the circumstances?)
2. How does holding on to that thought support you in maintaining your current identity?
3. Who would you become if you released the thought?

CHAPTER 5

Release It All to the Law

I made all of this out of nothing.
Trust me: I can take care of you.

—GOD

In many ancient cultures, there were very strict edicts regarding adherence to the moral laws of the land. Behaviors in contradiction to the ethical standards of the community were considered egregious and were dealt with accordingly. A person found guilty of lying in a court of law could be subjected to the same punishment that had been issued to the individual against whom they had borne false witness—up to and including death. A pretty intense commitment to maintaining moral order, huh? But that was then. What about now? What happens to those who have perpetrated harm in some way? Do they go free?

Rest assured that they do not. No one ever gets away with anything. Just as there are natural laws that govern physical existence, there are spiritual laws that govern our humanity. And, just like the Law of Gravity, Divine Law is always in full effect. The Law of Cause and Effect—or reaping and sowing, as it is more commonly referenced—is the infinite and infallible Law through which Divine Intelligence operates. Whether one believes in it or is aware of the ways in which its outworking is taking place has no bearing. Ignorance of the Law is no excuse. Each one of us is held accountable, in full measure, for how we show up in the world. Every thought, motive, and desire sent forth (cause) returns as manifested consequence (effect). Wise women know that whatever is being dished out—whether divine or debased, and whether held in heart for ourselves or someone else—ultimately finds its way back home.

Justice is a function of divine love. It aims to support the unfoldment of higher consciousness, ever-expanding levels of awareness and self-mastery that transcend the limited purview of human understanding. The time that passes between when a cause is set in motion, and when it returns to be experienced as an effect, is a demonstration of the magnanimity of that love. Often the consequences of our actions are not immediately visited upon us. This can be a blessing or a curse depending on how this lull in time is utilized. The unwise, having experienced no immediate repercussions of their actions, often misinterpret the apparent lack of consequence as a free pass. They may think they've won a cosmic "get out of jail free" card, so they fail to correct course. If so, the erroneous patterns of thoughts and behaviors unfortunately persist. We see examples of this being played out in the public arena regularly, even though it's a phenomenon common to all and not just those whose actions are subject to public scrutiny. Do you recall the last breaking news story that you heard about someone whose pattern of abuses finally caught up with them? Yeah, I can think of a few examples too.

Despite watching these supersized reminders playing themselves out in public spaces over and over again, some personalities remain so high on their own hubris that they still can't break free. They keep playing in the same dirt, remaining oblivious to the accumulating stain—even after racking up a string of violations and witnesses substantial enough to warrant their own *New York Magazine* cover! This is dangerously pompous and unwise. Resist becoming entangled in your own hype. The Law is no respecter of persons. No one stands beyond divine reproof. Jimmy Cliff made it plain, "The harder they come, the harder they fall, one and all."

A wise woman recognizes time as a treasured gift. The interim period between when a cause is set in motion and when it returns as an effect presents an opportunity to work some things out spiritually. Our aim must always be to transcend the levels of consciousness governed by our lower nature, which has gotten us into trouble in the first place. As our level of spiritual understanding increases, our behaviors align to reflect a deeper knowing. That's why this journey focuses so heavily on contemplation. We must become adept at looking at ourselves and examining our intentions and the impact of our actions with the wisdom of a loving, honest, and impartial observer. Doing so cultivates humility and facilitates healing. Awareness of the Law need not invoke fear, but it should inspire a healthy sense of reverence.

You may be balking at the idea of releasing it *all* to the unerring Law of Life, mistakenly believing that doing so would render you powerless to act. You may even think doing so renders you mute in the resolution of your own affairs. Nothing could be further from the truth. "Releasing it all to Divine Law" doesn't mean subjecting yourself to being violated by others. Setting appropriate boundaries, expecting fair treatment, and pursuing justice are keystones of personal responsibility that should not be abdicated. It's what healthy people do. Nor does it mean refraining from seeking appropriate recourse in the world of affairs, if that's what is warranted by your situation. Rather, this is about releasing your heart from the burden and bondage of contempt and unforgiveness—trusting, instead, that the operating principles of the universe are inerrant and unfailing, and knowing that the same force that created *all of this* can be trusted to right any wrong that has assailed you.

The ability to move in the direction of life's purpose is impeded when we're bogged down with anger and a need for revenge after being aggrieved in some way. This is especially true in those instances where we feel we've been violated and that justice has not been meted out. Some horror has ridden roughshod and unrepentant through our lives, and the urge to "clap back" has taken hold in a most formidable way. Without adequate inner grounding, we run the risk of getting caught up in routes that take us off course. This is the lesson that Yasmine learned on her journey.

YAZ'S STORY: FREEDOM THROUGH RELEASE

Yasmine is among the most brilliant, funny, and insightful people I've ever known. We met as patrons of a local nail salon, where we easily laughed and talked as our heels were buffed and our toes were painted. It was our shared love of old-school house, classic hip-hop, and straight-ahead jazz that sparked our friendship. Whenever our schedules allowed, we would catch a performance together. Beforehand, we would meet for dinner to catch up on the latest happenings in our personal and professional lives.

When Yaz's father became seriously ill, she struggled in deciding what to do. Her heart was clear that back home with her family was where she wanted to be, but her head weighed other considerations: *What about your career and the condo? Are you really going to press pause on a budding relationship with a really great guy?* Within months, Yaz had moved back to her hometown to assist with her father's care. Fortunately, she landed a fantastic position as the executive director of a respected nonprofit. At first, the transition was somewhat challenging, but before long Yaz found her rhythm and settled into being back in the community where she'd grown up. She poured herself into her job and the caretaking responsibilities that she shared with her family. Toward the end of the first year in her new position, Yaz began to confide that she was experiencing challenges with one of the women who sat on the board of the nonprofit where she worked. She wasn't quite sure why, but this woman just didn't seem to connect with her. Despite receiving accolades for the positive organizational transformation launched under her leadership, this particular board member would often find a way to minimize Yaz's accomplishments. The more commendations that Yaz received, the more obvious the board member's displeasure became. It was nothing extraordinarily overt—just a steady stream of nice-nasty jabs. At first she brushed off the board member's behavior, thinking that if she worked harder on building the relationship, she could win her over as an ally. After all, the performance of the organization was improving, the funders were pleased, and the staff had become more engaged under Yaz's leadership. She made an earnest attempt, but things didn't play out as Yaz had hoped. The board member's shady behavior persisted.

One midafternoon the phone rang, and it was clear that something was wrong. The distress was palpable when I heard Yaz's voice on the line. I worried that her dad had taken a turn for the worse, but that's not what had rattled her. Yaz was calling from her car, having just finished lunch with another board member who had given her a heads-up: A conversation was underway about whether or not she was a "good fit" for the organization and the direction it was headed. She was livid! There was no surprise when it was revealed that her detractor was spearheading these conversations. Yaz was shell-shocked. Yes, she knew that there had been tension, but she was completely blindsided by the deliberate effort being made to undermine her career. After all, she'd worked hard to prove herself, and the organization was making good strides. Questions were swirling: How long had this been going on? Why hadn't the other board members spoken up?

The next few weeks were like outtakes from a poorly crafted reality TV show. It seemed that every decision she made was subjected to new levels of scrutiny, and Yaz began defending herself and her work to anyone who would listen. She allowed her focus to shift away from being the most effective leader that she could be, and she grew consumed with managing the politics of her position instead. The longer this went on, the more resentful and miserable she became. Yaz had been trapped somewhere between anger and fear, and couldn't let go.

Yaz's breakthrough came one evening while she was visiting her parents. She had become so emotionally wrought by the turmoil of the previous weeks that her energy was depleted. As she moped about, her mom asked that she join her in the kitchen. As they sat having tea, Yaz's mom shared that her dad's most recent test results hadn't shown any signs of improvement and that the doctors had agreed that all treatment options had been exhausted. Yaz was devastated—not only about her father's prognosis, but also because she had been so busy amid the drama at her job that she had forgotten about her dad's series of follow-up tests. As she later explained, from that night on she released all attachment to the foolishness at her place of employment and began to focus on what really mattered! There was no more staying late to prove her dedication, no more working in overdrive to win allies. There was no more giving away of her power. She went in, gave her best, and rededicated her attention to what had brought her home in the first place: being present with her family during a very sacred time. She let go of anything that would have disrupted her devotion to purpose.

KNOWING WHAT THE ANCIENTS KNEW

Remaining firmly rooted in higher truth while enduring unfair criticism or undergoing unjust persecution can be daunting. Indeed, this is why the ancient wisdom outlined in the Kemetic (Egyptian) Virtues of Maat included "being free from resentment under the experience of persecution" and "under the experience of wrong" among the virtues that must be mastered in order to achieve enlightenment. According to Kemetic belief, enlightenment meant the full realization of oneness with God: living in alignment with the Universal Cosmic Law. The Virtues of Maat were part of the broader system of social and moral edicts around which this ancient civilization was organized. Our predecessors, who inhabited the planet thousands of years before us, were working to overcome the finite nature of humanity just as we are. There is much to be learned from the guidance that has been passed down across cultures and over time.

Who among us hasn't experienced some version of the "dry bones in the valley" situation that Yaz had to navigate? To a greater or lesser degree, we've each encountered people and situations that were unfair. Yaz never discovered the origin of the board member's disdain for her. There was no clear cause stemming from their interactions. Sometimes there are no easy answers to why people show up and act out the way that they do. In some cases, your presence alone is enough to trigger others. It's easy to get lost in the muck and mire of these situations. Yaz chose freedom, and things worked out for her. When the time came around, the board voted to renew her contract. Was it a unanimous vote? No. But the majority of the board members supported her, which was enough to silence her detractor.

What about you? What does it take for you to see the big picture of your life clearly enough not to become distracted by the upsets that happen along the journey? Is there anything you're holding on to that would be better addressed if released? The wise woman understands that every situation, especially those that cause angst, come bearing an opportunity to facilitate growth—a chance to recognize and release those aspects of our human nature that do not serve the awakened womanhood seeking to emerge through us. When we choose to trust in the perfect outworking of Divine Law, and when we seek guidance from the elevated consciousness within, our perspective shifts away from the emotional charge of the situation and toward a vision of the highest outcome. Release doesn't strip away the power to act. Rather, it empowers us with the peace of mind and heightened insight needed to set clear intentions and determine what actions, if any, should be taken.

We've all been aggrieved, and we've all caused some grief somewhere. No one is absolute in the expression of good or bad. We are complex and often contradictory beings. Few among us would be able to withstand the kind of tit-for-tat justice that we often feel others deserve. Where would it leave us if all we got back from life was an equal measure of what we've put out there, without ever being the beneficiaries or bestowers of grace? We release by trusting that nothing is ever lost in Divine Mind. We understand that we won't always see the outworking of justice within a timeframe or in a manner that satisfies human sensibilities. And we're fine with that because we know that how God handles God's business is none of our business. Thank you, God!

MEDITATIVE THOUGHT

I release and I let go. Divine Law is in full effect in my life.

WISDOM PROTOCOL

Think about an instance when you either willingly released a situation or were forced to do so. What were the circumstances and what was the outcome? Did this experience strengthen or weaken your resolve to release it all to the Law? Write about it in your journal or discuss it with a friend.

CHAPTER 6

Cats Don't Bark, Dogs Don't Meow, and People Can Only Be Who They Are

I am me. Take me as I am, or watch me as I go.

—UNKNOWN

It's tempting to become disappointed when people don't show up in our lives behaving in the manner that we expected or hoped they would. Whenever this occurs, one of two things is happening. Either we've forgotten that people are only capable of showing up as who they are, or we're treating them like extras in our life scripts, expecting them to eagerly play the part we've assigned them. Despite our wishing, wanting, and ranting, folks just keep showing up as themselves! Wise women know that this is precisely as it should be, and they wouldn't want life to unfold in any other way.

Zara often expressed disillusionment and frustration about the predictable ebb and flow of her relationship with Kevin, her companion of three years. She shared that on some days he treated her as if she was golden, and on other days as if she was the root cause of all of his pain. Because she "loved" him and was certain that he was the man for her, she magnified their fleeting moments of bliss and tried with all of her mental might, to dismiss the other 99.5 percent of their relationship. She focused her attention on figuring out what she could do differently to inspire more consistent demonstrations of loving behavior on his part. Yet, despite her increasingly creative efforts, the pattern continued. One day she was the center of Kevin's world; the next day he barely seemed to care that she existed. Still, she believed that he'd change. So she cried, prayed, and stayed, waiting for him to realize what a "good thing" they had. Then, one day, he had mercy on both of them and ended the relationship.

Zara lost it! She was enraged that he'd failed to honor her as a smart, creative, and caring woman, yet she couldn't see the dishonor she had repeatedly heaped upon him and herself. Her disconnect was so profound that she was *shocked* when he walked out. She was the only one who was surprised. Everyone else saw this coming from the next galaxy. Zara was so caught up rolling in the deep of her hurt and anger that she couldn't see that she wasn't grieving her relationship with Kevin; she was mourning the relationship she'd longed for that had remained unfulfilled. Think about it: Would anyone seeking love really want to be in a relationship with someone who could not, or would not, reciprocate that love? Kevin's physical departure was entirely congruent with the gaping bouts of emotional absence he'd demonstrated throughout the relationship. What Zara really wanted was a different man—a loving, caring man who would adore her and partner in relationship with her. At the time, Kevin was being true to his emotionally vacant self. But Zara, blinded by her desire for a happy future, couldn't really see him at all. How often do we willfully choose not to see the reality in front of us? What are the consequences?

Until Zara experiences a shift in awareness about who *she's* being, she will continue auditioning different men and trying to retrofit them to match the image in her magic mental mirror. Unless Zara successfully decodes her complicity in the demise of her relationship, she'll have difficulty relating to others as anything more than a distorted image of who she desires them to be. Needless to say, her cycle of pain and disappointment will continue to circle.

Wise women know that it's crucial to see people clearly and to accept them for who they are. Wise women understand that whether what others show us about themselves is a close match or distant variation of what we are hoping to see, we don't argue with the reality of who's in front of us. We acknowledge that the people in our lives don't owe us anything other than the truth of who they are at that moment in time. And that's good, because that's all they can give us anyway. What about you? Are there areas of your life where your inner wisdom is urging you to take a second look and perhaps see someone or something more clearly?

Are you someone who, like Zara, gets blinded by the fog of wishful thinking? If so, applying The Clarity Process is a helpful practice that you can incorporate immediately to see through situations more clearly.

Here's how things might have looked if Zara had completed The Clarity Process to distinguish between the *wish-ality* and *reality* of her relationship with Kevin.

- **Step 1: Name the thing that you want to examine.** Zara aspired to be in a loving relationship with Kevin, so a *loving relationship* is the thing that she would have named.

- **Step 2: Define its distinguishing attributes.** Next, Zara would have defined what being in a loving relationship meant to her. Let's suppose that she assigned the attributes *commitment*, *presence* (i.e., being there for each other and spending time together), and *caring* to her definition. These are the attributes that define how *she* desires to experience a loving relationship.

- **Step 3: Measure the degree to which those attributes are present or absent.** Next, Zara would have reflected on her relationship with Kevin and measured the degree to which commitment, presence, and caring were present or absent. She might have recalled that when she initiated a talk about their future together and transitioning from a casual to a committed relationship, Kevin had stated that he wasn't quite ready to "take it there." *Hmmm.* When looking for examples of presence and caring, Zara probably would have agreed that Kevin actually came around quite a bit. They spent time together each week. Still, she would likely have questioned why she and Kevin rarely socialized outside of their respective homes. And, why she had no meaningful interactions with his family or friends. And, even more importantly, why she rarely felt listened to or heard when sharing something important with him. As Arsenio would say, there were lots of "things that make you go hmmm."

- **Step 4: Treat the thing like what it is—and not what you'd hoped it would be, or what it proclaims to be.** After measuring the reality of what she was experiencing against the attributes that she'd defined as being most important, Zara may have concluded that her *situationship* with Kevin didn't possess the requisite qualities of a *loving relationship*, even though that's what she desired. From that point on she would have been empowered to treat the situationship like what it was and manage her expectations accordingly. Maybe she would have shared her insights with Kevin and inquired about how he saw their relationship. Perhaps she would have clearly articulated her desire for a loving relationship and extended an opportunity for Kevin to respond and share what he was seeking. From a place of clarity, the couple may have aligned and decided to move forward together. Or, they may have realized that their visions were incompatible and agreed to part ways. Either way, Zara wouldn't have been so blindsided by her attachment to her desires that she couldn't see what was right in front of her. Being radically honest with herself early on may have mitigated the pain of incongruence that she experienced when her *wish-ality* collided with the reality of her relationship with Kevin.

Seeing clearly liberates you to choose a course of action that is more likely to produce the results that you truly desire. It frees us from the perils of walking through life with blinders on and then remaining non-responsive when we bump into evidence that contradicts what we wish to be true. It frees others from the tyranny of our judgment when they refuse to play the role that we've tried to impose on them. Most of all, clear vision empowers us to see the pathway toward people and experiences that are authentically in alignment with the happiness that we seek. That's why The Clarity Process is so useful! Lock it in for future reference and apply it as often as needed. Wise women know that cats don't bark, dogs don't meow, and people can only be who they are.

MEDITATIVE THOUGHT

I release false expectations. I embrace clarity.
And I am set free.

WISDOM PROTOCOL

Bring to mind someone whom you feel has disappointed you in some way. They've failed to meet some expectation that you held for them. Then, spend some time unpacking your disappointment. What's at the core of it? Is your expectation one that the other person shares? Have you clearly communicated your needs and/or desires? What happens if this individual is unable or unwilling to change? Can you accept what is, or will you have to release? Either way, how will you find peace?

CHAPTER 7

Overcoming a Culture of "Something for Nothing"

Good planning and hard work lead to prosperity,
but hasty shortcuts lead to poverty.
—PROVERBS 21:5

The illusion of overnight success permeates our culture. Almost every other person you meet is riding the tide of the latest "new" thing that promises to elevate her (and you, too, if you'll just place an order for $19.95) to the next level of prosperous living at warp speed. The promise of a hasty rise to the top have been bolstered by throngs of "spiritual leaders", prosperity preachers and assorted gurus who specialize in the mass dissemination of information on spiritual technology. In some instances these actions were actually well intended, but most were incomplete. Consequently, throngs of people became excited about the possibility of simply creating a vision for a better life and—poof!—having it magically appear in the not-too-distant future. Multitudes of vision boards were created. Affirmations were affixed to mirrors across the globe, and meditation mats grew worn and discolored from the imprints of hopeful human behinds that sat far too long, waiting on their miracle of choice to fall from the sky. Many became disenchanted when little or nothing happened and began to doubt the veracity of the technologies they'd embraced. The problem wasn't that the tools were ineffective, but that the understanding of how to use them was incomplete.

Of course, prayer, meditation, vision boards, affirmations, and other tools of enlightenment are important components of an abundant spiritual life. But their purpose must be clearly understood. They are instruments designed to assist us in raising the level of consciousness to actually align with the desires and intentions of Infinite Mind that are seeking expression through us. They help us to move beyond the limitations of the human mind and tap into that of the higher mind, the God Consciousness that dwells within. This is a vital first step in achieving the demonstration of any idea in the material world.

But you can't ignore what comes next. After you've been infused with the divine idea, you must take deliberate action. You must follow the inner urging that is seeking to guide your steps. Don't be discouraged because you can't see exactly how things are going to unfold. Just make a solid plan and begin moving your feet. As you are obedient and persistent in your actions, the unseen forces of the universe will ensure that the right people, places, and situations will show up as needed. You are in partnership with the Divine for the unfoldment of every righteous dream and desire of your heart. Rest assured, there is no godly assist for desires of a carnal nature that have no purpose other than to fulfill the hunger of the human ego. If the desire is selfish or would cause harm to another, you're on your own. Albeit true, this bit of wisdom contradicts much of what we hear and see happening in the world around us.

THAT'S THE WAY OF THE WORLD

Kick. Claw. Lie. Cheat. Steal. Kill. By any means necessary, "get yours." You deserve it. These are the incessant urgings of a world rooted in fear. And a world dangerously ignorant of the spiritual laws that govern existence. The rules of engagement in this world are simple: do what you must in order to come out on top. Don't worry about who you step on or the carnage that you create along the way. Ask for forgiveness later. But what the world won't tell you is that ill-gotten gains won't last. They can't. No matter how much someone tries to justify having acted unjustly towards others in order to hasten their own rise, it won't erase the cosmic debt accrued when those dastardly deeds were committed. There may be the temporary high of winning the spoils, but in the end nothing attained by ill-gotten gains will endure. The same mind and heart that secured the "win" calls forth its ruin. A larcenous heart is its own demise. Don't be deceived. Life *always* answers who we are.

Remember that Divine Law is in effect in all things, including the manifestation of your dreams and desires. It can't be manipulated for service to anything that is in opposition to its all-good nature. There are no magic fixes. Work is required on both the spiritual and earthly planes. But when we act in concert with the Divine, the reward is immeasurable. Sometimes the unfoldment of our life's purpose is hindered because we resist making the changes required to grow into the person whom we must become in order to fulfill that mission. "It's hard to face yourself and see all of your inadequacies, shortcomings, and addictions staring back at you," says Share, who has embraced the philosophy of Nichiren Buddhism for over forty years. "In Buddhism we face those things head-on. It's only through the process of coming face-to-face with yourself that you are able to change in spite of yourself." Here again, we are reminded that "something for nothing" fantasies won't get us to the promised land of purposeful living. We've got to put in the work.

Many times we resist the path of self-exploration and growth because we've experienced, or witnessed through our observation of others, just how rocky that road can be! We pray for a new life, a divinely inspired life, and then everything begins to fall apart. The job, the house, the relationship, the car, and the five-year plan all decide to take a road trip to hell! Any or all aspects of the life we're transitioning from may undergo adjustments or complete overhauls as our new lives are taking form. Rest easy. This doesn't mean that anything is wrong. It's just the acid jazz rhythm of life being recalibrated. Anticipating these upsets and knowing how to process them is vital to keeping feelings of overwhelm at bay when things go topsy-turvy.

What's your go-to practice for regaining a sense of calm when faced with some manner of upset? How do you access the "peace be still" part of yourself needed to navigate the rough waters of life? For Share, chanting, along with morning and evening prayers focused on gratitude are pathways to inner peace. "These practices help to refocus the heart and mind on higher truths and strengthen the resolve not to yield to difficulty," she avows. The ways in which we summon the wisdom and deep peace that are part of our spiritual DNA are as varied as we are. What's important is knowing and engaging in the disciplined practice of whatever works for you. Perhaps it's a fasting regimen. Or perhaps burning off upset energy through vigorous exercise helps you to restore calm. Maybe it's a quick getaway to a serene location where you can clear your thoughts. Or it could be a long conversation with your favorite auntie who always knows just what to say to help you bring your life back into proper perspective. If you haven't yet discovered which practices strengthen you the most, invest time in doing so. It is a worthwhile endeavor that will pay off many times over.

If we're honest with ourselves, most of us would prefer that the pathway to our brighter tomorrows be smooth, well-lit, and constructed for maximum comfort. Some small part of us may even feel that we deserve it. After all, we're good people trying to do the right thing. Yet our inner wisdom reminds us that anything worth having is worth the work and the wait required. You've probably heard the old saying, "What comes easy won't always last. And what lasts won't always come easy." Knowing this, we are not dissuaded when we encounter potholes, detours, and maybe even a few gale-force winds. Wise women are committed to overcoming the culture of something for nothing. We do not retreat to familiar comforts when things feel a bit uncomfortable. We continue moving forward, remaining true to the course. The pay-off makes it all worthwhile. In the end, you'll see the most real self-help guru you'll ever find each time that you look in the mirror.

MEDITATIVE THOUGHT

I am willing to put in the work required
to live the life I desire.

WISDOM PROTOCOL

Reflect on a time in your life when things seemed unsettled or uncertain. In what ways did the experiences of that season empower you to be the person you are today? Who or what helped you to persevere through those challenging times?

CHAPTER 8

Who Have You Had Your Mouth on Lately?

Raise your words, not your voice. It is rain that grows flowers, not thunder.

—RUMI

In the nomenclature of today's popular culture, "gossip" is a catch-all term used to describe everything from idle tidbits about the lives of celebrities to the benign chitchat among friends. Gossiping has become an accepted social pastime, bolstered by media outlets dedicated to its perpetuation. But the real, adverse impact of gossip in our personal lives isn't nearly as titillating as the tabloids and late-night TV shows would suggest. Gossip takes on several forms: outright lies, half truths, and whole truths that don't need to be told by the person speaking them. Those who contend, "If it's true, it's not gossip," are in error. Having knowledge of someone else's business, true or not, doesn't mean it's yours to mind. The various forms of gossip are held together by a single thread—the underlying intent to cause harm.

Gossiping, as discussed here, is the slanderous whispering about someone that is intended to diminish that person's standing among others. Gossiping is an act of spiritual warfare that uses words as the weapon of choice. The gossiper doesn't bring information to you as a simple FYI. Rather, there is a deliberate intent to negatively influence your thoughts and feelings about the person who is the target of gossip. Whether the gossip is cloaked in casualness, feigned concern, or humor makes no difference. It's a verbal and spiritual hit that carries consequences for all involved. People rarely gossip about those who are drowning alongside them in the cesspool of spiritual mediocrity. Rather, their venom is most often reserved for those who stand out because they are flying high in some way. Who you have to become to wade knee-deep and uninvited in other people's business isn't who you must become to live a purpose-filled life.

HAIL TO THE QUEEN

Most of us have come across at least one chronic gossiper in our lifetime. Once I knew someone who could have been crowned queen of the gossiper's coven. Her tongue was lightning, utterly indiscriminate in whom it struck. Friends, foes, family, coworkers, neighbors—everyone was fair game. You were "her girl" as long as you were sitting in front of her, but the minute you turned your back, you became a target. On any given day, if you were sitting at a table with a group of her *friends* or family members, you could break into a freestyle cypher filled with details about each of their lives that they had no idea you knew. Anyone at the table could do the same! That's how this chick rolled. She wasn't keen on fact-checking. As long as the story was salacious, she would ensure that it was in circulation.

Gossiping wasn't merely a pastime; it had become her vocation. If she was jealous, she talked about you. If she was mad, she talked about you. If she was bored, she talked about you. If she wasn't getting enough attention or felt that you were getting too much attention, she talked about you. If it was a sunny day and all was well with the world, she'd talk about you. Sometimes gossiping was merely how she made conversation. Gossiping was her catch-all social currency. Her assaults generally came gift-wrapped as humor. But behind each loud cackle was pain—her own and that which she inflicted on others. Completely innocent bystanders, deeply hurt by the flat-out lies and innuendo she spread about their loved ones, were collateral damage amid her emotionally wounded gangsta girl drive-bys. One-by-one, over time, people who were once close to her faded into the distance once the radioactivity of her words began to burn too deeply.

Some people are too wounded to love in ways that are healthy. You don't have to stop loving them, but sometimes it's wise to love them from a distance. Stop accepting invitations to dine at tables where the condition for being seated is that your dignity be left behind. You *know* that you deserve better! When a situation no longer uplifts you, supports your growth, or brings you joy—respect yourself enough to let it go.

CHECK, CHECK, CHECK YOURSELF BEFORE YOU WRECK YOURSELF . . .

Granted, most gossipers don't rival the queen, but at some point we've each served in her court. We've discussed business that wasn't ours and passed on talk to others that we weren't certain was true. We've remained silent when we should have nipped destructive conversation in the bud. We've gossiped. And, we each became a bit smaller every time that we did. In most instances, you're playing one of three roles when gossiping is taking place, and there are release remedies for each. If you're the gossiper, realize that the target of your attack is not the source of your pain. Work instead to uncover the true nature of what's bothering you, and turn your attention to healing the wounds of your discontent. Examine the type of psychological or social payoff that you get from gossiping. Does it make you feel important, or like you're "in the know"? Is there some part of you that feels better about your situation when you can talk about someone else's situation? Is your verbal lashing symptomatic of some silent resentment or envy that you harbor against the person you're talking about? *What's your skin in the game?* Figure out what motivates the lashings of your tongue and then do the inner work necessary to heal your hurt and eliminate the destructive behavior.

If you are on the receiving end of gossip about someone else, refuse to collude. Being a receptacle for gossip perpetuates both the unhealthy behavior of the gossiper and continued harm to the target. Instead, demonstrate spiritual courage by refusing to be a haven for gossip. Just say, "This isn't the type of conversation that I want to have. Let's talk about something else." When you allow the gossiping to continue unchecked, you act as an accessory. There is no such thing as being an innocent bystander when you are a silent witness to someone being attacked. If you find that you are frequently on the receiving end of a gossiper's rant, ask yourself, *Why does the gossiper feel so comfortable coming to me?* People are actually pretty selective about where they spread their mess. There are some people in the gossiper's realm of orbit whom she would never dare to approach with the pettiness that she readily delivers to your doorstep. Why might that be the case? Sometimes we unwittingly communicate our availability for experiences that we profess to abhor by being passive participants. Don't allow yourself to be used in this way.

If you're being gossiped about, do what's necessary to guard your heart. It's difficult not to let the hurtful words of others find refuge in your innermost being, but it's essential that you do not allow this to happen. Instead of rushing out to defend yourself or engaging in battle with your attacker, go within. Steep yourself in Truth. Be emboldened by the divine call on your life and continue moving forward in answer to that call. Remain focused on where you're headed. Don't allow yourself to be distracted or derailed by the mindless chatter of others.

The weaponization of words—in the form of lies, slander, backbiting, harassment, and gossip—is often levied as punishment for breaking rank and moving beyond the imposed limits of the status quo. The college student whose classmate posted a vicious and embarrassing lie about her on Facebook the day after it was announced that she had been awarded a prestigious scholarship. The nurse whose co-workers ostracized her and began whispering negatively about her when she applied and was accepted into medical school. The Somali-American legislator who was taunted and harassed by a D.C. taxi driver who called her "ISIS" and threatened to take off her hijab. These are real-life examples of social shots fired in retaliation for upsetting the status quo, for moving beyond the limits that others sought to impose. It's one of the ways that those who feel threatened by your expansion may try to compel you to "stay in your place" or use to retaliate when it becomes clear that you have absolutely no intention of doing so. It's punishment for triggering the dark fears of inadequacy in others by simply walking in the brilliance of your own light.

What is the wise woman to do in the midst of this socialized insanity? Devote yourself to doing the inner work necessary to remain spiritually and emotionally grounded. This will enable you to see through the feckless antics of others and rise above the upsets created by the lower-level energies that you may encounter. And, always—always—be mindful of how you use words. Once during an interview, Mari Evans—the renowned Black Arts Movement poet—was asked a leading question that she interpreted as an invitation to be critical of someone. Evans wisely replied, "Thank you for that question, but I don't want to address that. I wouldn't want to comment on anything in the direction you just headed. That's not the sound that I'd want to leave behind me." Her response was golden! We would each be wise to live up to her example by being mindful of the sounds that we leave behind.

Wise women understand that meaningful and courageous conversations *with* those who are a part of our intimate circle add far greater value than talking *about* them behind their backs ever could. We must commit to being principled in our relationships with one another. Together, we must model the mature womanhood and sisterhood that we each desire and deserve. Now let your resident gossiper run and go tell *that*!

MEDITATIVE THOUGHT

Today I raise my words and keep them lifted. I am mindful of the sounds that I leave behind.

WISDOM PROTOCOL

Decide today that you will not be a party to gossip. Preparation is empowering. Determine now how you will respond the next time a person attempts to verbally slay someone in your presence. What will you say and do to make it clear that you won't be complicit?

CHAPTER 9

When Things Fall Apart

When God is going to do something wonderful, He or She always starts with a hardship; when God is going to do something amazing, He or She starts with an impossibility.

—ANNE LAMOTT

Sometimes poor judgment and bad choices lead us to very tough experiences. Or our lives collide with the sickness harbored in another's mind and heart, which hurls us into a situation rife with agony and discontent. The footprint of the liars, manipulators, and abusers we've encountered can often be seen well after their physical presence is no longer a part of our lives. Maybe life itself deals the blow, thrusting us into a dungeon of despair with no one else to blame. A difficult diagnosis or a poor prognosis can easily leave even the most resilient among us numb. What, then, are we to make of being cast into such desolate places? What purpose does such darkness serve? How do we restore ourselves to a level of functioning that places us in alignment with the Divine within?

No matter how you get there, being in the dungeon is not easy. When you're in the dungeon, there's no "Hallelujah Chorus" being sung in the background. No. It's damp, dark, and colder than a Siberian winter. The air is stifled and musty, and there are no soft places to rest your head. The only sounds you hear are your own strangled screams crying for relief. These disquieting challenges take on many faces. After many years of loving and living with someone, you find yourself unexpectedly going it alone. Your money runs out before your financial needs do. The body you've cared for is suddenly overwrought with illness. In those moments, you're not feeling blessed by the "opportunity." Not in that moment, and often not for some time. Yet if we acknowledge the presence of the Divine in all things, we must also accept that even in our darkest hours, we are not alone. This allows us to trust that through the divine alchemy of Spirit, even our greatest pain plays a mission-critical role in equipping us to live a fuller expression of life. Indeed, if it weren't for some of the dungeon experiences, we wouldn't be prepared to complete the work we were born to do.

BEAUTY FOR ASHES IN AVALON VILLAGE

Highland Park, Michigan, is a small city that literally sits within the city of Detroit. Once a vibrant community, economically bolstered by the presence and financial boon of the Ford and Chrysler corporations, the city has steadily declined in population and prosperity over the past several decades. The three-square-mile expanse once known as The City of Trees now stands as a remnant of its former self. While there has been commercial development along the city's main street, many of the adjoining residential streets haven't been beneficiaries of the same care. To many observers, the city resembles an urban ghost town simply too recalcitrant to take its final bow. But through the eyes of Shamayim Harris, lovingly known as Mama Shu, a higher vision was formed and is now becoming a reality.

Where some saw vacant lots and abandoned buildings, she saw possibility. Where some saw despair, she saw hope and opportunity. Where others looked out and saw vast nothingness, Mama Shu decided she'd build a self-sustaining eco-village. "I've always been able to see a thing past its ugliness or superficiality. This place was unloved," she shares. In Mama Shu's love-fueled vision, the vacant lot was a perfect spot for a community garden and urban green space. The abandoned house next door would be transformed into The Homework House, a place where neighborhood children would gather to share in nutritionally dense meals while continuing their studies. Shipping containers would be rebirthed as The Goddess Marketplace, an entrepreneurial center led by women artisans. Beyond the renovated structures and carefully manicured lawns, Mama Shu holds an even higher vision for the people of Avalon Village: "I envision people becoming motivated, hopeful, and empowered by what's happening here. It's important that we understand the power of what's possible when we come together to create the quality living experiences that we deserve."

The material manifestation of Avalon Village didn't happen overnight. This is often the case with big visions. They must simmer and stew in consciousness for a bit before becoming ready to be brought into form. For several years, Mama Shu sat with her vision of creating a vibrant, happy community with safe spaces for learning and healing, allowing it to expand. During this season she took small steps. She hosted fish fry fund-raisers. She began to purchase land—all while simultaneously fulfilling the roles of mother, community activist, and educational administrator. Most of all, she remained "in the mix" by consistently being present among her neighbors and sharing her vision so that others could catch hold of it. Ultimately, things came together magnificently. But before they came together, things fell apart.

As a loving mom, Shamayim's greatest fear was of something happening to one of her four children. Mothers the world over can attest to the deep and abiding concern for the well-being of their children, which is coded into our DNA. Mama Shu was brought face-to-face with that fear when her two-year-old son, Jakobi Ra, died in a hit-and-run car accident. As she reeled from the pain of such profound loss, she came upon a book that framed grief as "love with no place to go."

That idea connected with Shamayim, who knew—at her core—that she was being called upon to channel her love into the community redevelopment project that had been within her for quite some time. Feeling the loving presence of her son and other ancestors has strengthened and emboldened her. "Do more," they have encouraged her. "Go on, Shamayim." And that's precisely what she's done.

In addition to her own home, Mama Shu has purchased numerous other properties on the block and continued beautification efforts. She created Jakobi Ra Park to honor the memory of her son. Once Mama Shu was in motion, bringing her Spirit-inspired vision to life, gale force blessings began to rush in. Mama Shu and the Avalon Village Project have attracted supporters around the globe! As phase one of the four-phase project nears completion, over $243,000 has been raised via a crowdfunding campaign, and $100,000 prefab Cocoon9 house has been gifted by *The Ellen DeGeneres Show*. Countless others have sown into this grand vision. Skilled tradesmen, artists, farmers, activists, engineers, and futurists are among those who have come together to demonstrate the power of collective work and responsibility in self-determined communities. The Avalon Village Project stands as testimony that gentrification and displacement aren't the only solutions for revitalizing challenged urban communities. It's scheduled to be completed by 2020. You can keep up with Mama Shu and the villagers by visiting www.theAvalonVillage.org.

There's something sacred about traversing through and ascending from life's dungeons. The journey changes you at the core. At first, you might not be able to put your finger precisely on what it is, but you feel the difference in the depths of your soul. Some conversations you're simply not willing to have anymore. Some people you're not interested in spending as much time with as before. Some places you're just not interested in going. You learn to keep yourself clothed in the appropriate spiritual attire (compassion, kindness, humility, gentleness, patience, and forgiveness) and are kept dry. You master layering your prayers and remain warm. No longer do you become unsteady when darkness looms, because you recognize your power to be "the light" in all situations. Resting in the soft, sweet embrace of Spirit, you remain refreshed and renewed.

The mystical alchemy of the dungeon experience assures us that no matter how deep the hurt or how far the fall, through the healing, transmuting power of the Most High, good emerges from even the most challenging seasons. Those experiences shape and mold us. The disequilibrium that caused the shift in the world around us also causes a change within us. Mama Shu reflects that she's become more open and receptive as a result of her journey: "I'm more submissive to Spirit. There's no pushing or shoving to try and make things happen. Instead, I relax. I just honor and respect what's coming through." Every experience from the moment you were born through this holy instant plays a vital role in molding you into a wise woman who, because of her experiences and not despite them, is able to fully express the highest intention for her life.

Be gentle with yourself while you're on this path. Avoid holding yourself to the impossibly high standard of always getting things right. You will not. No one does.

Center yourself in Spirit and watch how the life force that created you shows up to support you and see you through. At this moment, your circumstance may feel like more than you can handle alone. The good thing is, you don't ever have to handle *anything* alone. The Most High is with you. When the cliff of adversity is high, wise women don't worry about falling off. They simply remember that they can fly.

MEDITATIVE THOUGHT

I release attachment to appearances. Confidently and courageously I move in the direction of my purpose.

WISDOM PROTOCOL

Write in your journal or have a conversation with someone about challenges you've overcome in the past. Reflect on how you felt when you were in the midst of the difficulty in contrast to how you felt once you reached the other side. Then name a character attribute that was cultivated or strengthened as a result of that experience.

CHAPTER 10

The Double Entendre: A Woman Out of Time

Some people are old at 18 and some are young at 90 . . . time is a concept that humans created.

—YOKO ONO

How many of us really believe that age is just a number? We allow so much of our lives to be governed by culturally imposed notions of time. Many of them are driven by archaic ideas that seek to dictate when and where we, as adult women, enter the various phases of our lives. What is it that makes one young or old anyway? Is it chronological age? Level of maturity? State of mind or heart? For decades, Hollywood has sought to put a shelf life on the appeal of female actors in lead roles, often relegating more mature actresses to supporting roles. But then life serves up the genius of Viola Davis and Meryl Steep, and the fallacy of those ideas cannot be denied. Brilliance magnetizes at any age. Witnessing the elegant movements of Carmen de Lavallade and the grace of Cicely Tyson on stage confirms that time is merely an illusion. Around the world, the incessantly loud ticking of biological clocks could be heard, sending many thirty-five-year-olds into a panic—until they witnessed what happened when Janet unplugged the clock and gave birth at fifty! The idea of time and our relationship to it is so fundamental to how we structure and engage life. Several years ago, I saw an advertisement for a women's retreat for which the theme was "A Woman Out of Time." Although I didn't participate in the retreat, I was intrigued by the title and began to ponder its meaning. Let's explore this concept together.

Are you a woman out of time? One who has removed herself from the snares of conventionally imposed notions about what should have been accomplished by a given time in life? Are you living free from the constraints of disbelief, fear, and the expectations of others that are rooted in ideas about time? Unbound by the commonly accepted limitations of time and space that seek to define you and place parameters on your possibilities based on the timestamp on your birth certificate? Or, are you a woman out of time—distraught by the thought of your human life running out before you've truly lived? Dying a little more each moment, as increasingly shallow breaths fill your body with regret about words unspoken, risks still untaken, and dreams continuously deferred? Was Langston Hughes right? Have your deferred dreams festered like rotten meat? Do they now sag "like a heavy load"? Are you joyously and expectantly living outside of the constraints of time? Or are you living in fear that time is running out? Which woman *out of time* are you?

You've seen her before. You instantly recognize her swagger as she glides into the room with graceful confidence, her sincere smile lighting up darkened places with each parting of her lips. She seems unfazed by the conditions around her that have other folks hot and bothered. Somehow she knows that despite appearances, everything is going to be all right. Never one to get caught up in other people's drama, she's busy living out ever-expanding expressions of her life's purpose. Sure, she's known heartbreak and failure, experienced loss, and managed her share of disappointments. But fortuitously, rather than leaving her broken, these experiences have added rich and deep texture to the tapestry of her life. Not lacking in decisiveness, she activates the "Tina Turner Rule" when confronted with people or situations that don't support her good. With fierce determination, she "clocks Ike" metaphorically and keeps it moving.

She enthusiastically says *yes* to life and willingly accepts responsibility for her happiness. She exudes warmth and is an encourager. Many are inspired by her. Some are even intimidated by her because they haven't yet figured out that the same magic they witness in her, and desperately covet, is alive and seeking expression through them. Time is her friend because she uses it wisely. It doesn't constrain her because she doesn't allow it to define her. Living into new dreams is a luxury that she regularly affords herself. She's not caught up in the useless folly of trying to be young. She's deeply rooted in being her ageless, timeless, and beautiful self. If you want to see her up close, look around you. Often the real wonders of the world don't make the front page of the newspaper. But she's right there in your office, on your block, or at your place of worship. Seek her out and let her know that you see her and admire her.

And you've met the other woman too. On the surface things may seem okay, but a look beneath her veil reveals a callous interior. Her saccharine smile attempts to hide the contempt she feels for herself and for others who, by their very living, have raised her ire. She, too, has experienced seasons of life wrought with emotional, material, physical, or spiritual pain. The harsh winds and bitter cold of those seasons have encouraged poisonous roots to grow into her experience as anger, doubt, jealousy, and insecurity. She is thinking: *Who does she think she is? Walking up in here like she Solange or something. She ain't hardly no Solange!* Her needle is stuck, endlessly replaying the refrain of "Another Somebody Done Somebody Wrong Song." She's perpetually disgruntled. The boss, the job, the kids, the man who didn't stay, the one who did, the friend who disappointed her, and an array of others who declined the character roles she'd attempted to cast them in get blamed for her unhappiness. *Being married to Harry has been the biggest waste of my damn time!* she says. *I should have run away when I had the chance.* Rather than stand on her own spiritual strength and accept responsibility for the outworking of her life's affairs, she is consumed with the useless folly of keeping tabs on debts she was never owed. *If I hadn't got stuck raising these hardheaded, greedy, ungrateful bastards, I could have really made something out of myself.*

She's walking and she's talking. On many days she can be caught creating various emanations of hell for herself and others, but she's actually in a deep slumber. Not yet awakened to the most profound truth of her being that exists unadulterated beyond the boundaries of her current understanding, she seeks with futility to find answers outside of herself that can only be found within her soul. But in the scheme of things, even that's all right. She is the child of a loving Creator who, whenever she's ready, will meet her right where she is and lead her home. In the meantime, our job is simply to keep her lifted in consciousness and get the china ready. Until she wakes up, time is her enemy—a moment-by-moment reminder of longings that have remained unfulfilled, an unforgiving master who continually reminds her of how far away she is from who she once dreamed of becoming.

As a young woman, I began to take note of the differences I observed in how more mature women conducted themselves in response to the passing of time. The distinct patterns that emerged have been profoundly instructive. There were those who served as solid examples of the type of woman I aspired to become. They taught me the value of expressing my higher self in a way that honors life and supports others in doing the same. They modeled what it means to be *in* this world, but not *of* it. Having freed themselves from the limitations of conventional notions of time, their courage, grace, and ageless beauty continue to inspire me. Equally meaningful were those who stood as poignant reminders of what happens if the business of healing and restoration is left undone. They, too, left an indelible impression.

Wisdom is a function of growth, not time. Some people are no more thoughtful and sagacious in their eighties than they were in their teens. Growing older does not guarantee becoming wiser. There's no surety that wisdom will emerge from experience either. Have you ever observed someone who has "been through the fires" of adversity yet come out on the other end as puffed up and foolish as when she went in? Trials are great teachers, but only for receptive students. Some people remain perched up on their own hubris until life comes back and drags them some more. We exist in a free will universe. It's up to us to choose how to harness the experiences we accumulate over our lifetimes. What's your truth? Which woman are you?

MEDITATIVE THOUGHT

I am ageless, fearless, and wonderfully made. I release any limiting thoughts about time. My purpose transcends the constraints of time.

WISDOM PROTOCOL

Explore your relationship with time by pondering the following questions: Is time "on your side," or is it something that seems to be "slipping away" from you? How would your life change if your relationship to time shifted?

CHAPTER 11

Seven Billion Souls on Board

A woman that knows her worth doesn't measure herself against another woman, but stands strong, calm, and self-confident.

—UNKNOWN

Imagine that you're a passenger on a crowded airplane, and each seat is inhabited by a fellow sojourner. As you place your carry-on in the overhead compartment, you notice all the different types of baggage stowed away. Now, snugly strapped into your seat, you look around the cabin at the myriad faces that surround you and observe that each is distinctly unique, yet all share common characteristics. You reflect on the fact that even though you're traveling together, your reasons for making the trip are as individualized as each of you. Though you're sharing the same flight, your experience will be different. Some will sleep while others commune with their electronic devices. Some will read while others chat. Some will be filled with peace while others will purchase a glass of wine to calm their nerves. Even though you're sharing an experience in time and space, everyone understands that getting to the shared destination won't happen in the same way for everyone. No one expects another passenger's plane ride to be exactly like his or her own. No one is upset by the variation. Onboard the Boeing 737, everyone seems to resonate with the Neo-Zen philosophy "Do you." Yet, for many, that philosophical grounding fades away as soon as the wheels touch the tarmac and the unholy trifecta—comparison, covetousness, and competition—once again reign supreme.

When we compare ourselves to others, we defy the wisdom of God in making us each unique. Comparison sets up the fatally false expectation that your life should mirror that of another human instead of being the out-picturing of God expressing distinctly through and as you. Whenever you're caught up in the stronghold of comparison, you will lose. Always. Somewhere there's a woman considered richer, smarter, prettier, or sweeter than you. Somewhere there's a woman who has the job, house, and car you'd hoped to have. She's happy, she's healthy, and her heart is at peace. She uses her talents in sacred service to others. At the end of each day, she goes home to exactly the kind of man you've been praying would enter your life. Nice picture, right?

In this moment, check in with yourself to see what feelings arose as you read the passage above. What thoughts come up when you think about an incredibly beautiful woman living an amazingly beautiful life? Do you find yourself disqualifying her life in some way? You may be thinking, *Who knows what type of suffering she's doing on the inside!* Or, does something inside of you say, *No way!* and dismiss the prospect as fantasy? After all, no one has it all. Whenever you find that your heart can only tolerate the possibility of another woman living a fully expressed life by contemplating what might *not* be working for her, know that it's likely a sign of a fundamental disconnect between the life you say you want and what you think is really possible. The hard realities of life visit everyone, so it's a given that she weathers storms like everyone else. But if your capacity to be happy for another woman can only be activated by the assurance that she's challenged in some way, it's important to recognize that as a call to explore where healing might be needed in your own life.

There's a classic scene in *The Color Purple* where the main character, Miss Celie, tells her son-in-law, Harpo, to beat his wife, Sophia. It's an abuse and betrayal that Celie has known all her life, and even though she knows it is wrong, she becomes complicit in the violation of another woman. Celie's response comes from a very dark and visceral place. In that moment, her consciousness seems to reflect this belief: *I've had to suffer, so why shouldn't she? If I can't have joy, she shouldn't either.* Have you ever witnessed one woman going Miss Celie on another in the real world?

Competition among women can be epic, and it can take some very bitter turns. The deeper the inner wounds, the more socially combative some women become in the quest for power, status, and control. Social theorists who have studied this phenomenon have termed it the Power Dead-Even Rule. In casual parlance, it's the unspoken rule that says, "Everything is good between us as long as everything is relatively the same between us." It shows up both in subtle and more profound ways. I witnessed this unfortunate social game being played out during a luncheon hosted by a local professional women's organization.

The eight women at our table were each bright and successful in their own right. As we dined, a couple of the women began to share highlights from their summer vacations. They'd each gone on fantastic voyages to distant lands. The group listened with excitement as they told of their adventures. One of our tablemates, Belle, is very well-known in the civic community due to her high-profile position in the foundation world. She joined the rest of us in celebrating the incredible vacation experiences that had been shared, but she didn't disclose what she'd done over the summer. Once the final, *oohs, ahhs,* and *wows* had been offered, one of the vacationers turned to Belle and said, “So, Belle, tell us what you did this summer. I’m sure you did something ab-so-lute-ly fabulous.” Belle demurred and moved the conversation along. *One time.* Before the main course ended, the happy vacationer directed her attention to Belle again: “I can’t believe you didn’t do anything *alllll* summer long.” Her comment was chased with yawping laughter. Meow! *Two times.* Just as the dessert was being placed before us, the vacation queen came for Belle a *third time.* This time, Belle acquiesced and spilled the beans on her vacation. And let me tell you, it was all kinds of wonderful—replete with family, friends, a secluded island, and personal chef! Hearing about Belle’s sojourn was exciting! The only thing missing at that moment was Robin Leach showing up to serve glasses of Ace of Spades champagne to enhance our listening pleasure. Most of the women at the table were thrilled to capture a glimpse into Belle’s world. We were genuinely happy to hear about her grand adventure. Interestingly enough, our previously chatty vacation queen didn’t seem quite as elated as the rest of us. She turned three shades of red—blush, blood, and brick—by the time that Belle finished her vacation update. She offered not one congratulatory word to Belle. Instead, she shoved that crème brûlée down her throat as if it were the last supper, apparently upset that her plan to upstage Belle had failed.

The vacation queen hadn’t pressed Belle for details about her vacation out of genuine interest. Rather, she erroneously thought that she’d seized an opportunity to best Belle. Her behavior was likely rooted in some form of competition that she’d constructed in her own mind. Just imagine the extraordinary pressure that women carry when they burden themselves with this type of baggage. Playing “one-up” is a girl’s game. Grown women should be beyond it. These behaviors signal insecurity or an overly competitive personality, and they are not demonstrative of the self-confidence possessed by women who are attuned to their inner wisdom. Wise women abide by the credo, “When I shine, you shine; and when you shine, I shine.” When your own inner light is aglow, there’s no desire to dim anyone else’s flame.

You get the idea. Maybe you've even experienced something similar. Perhaps you're *that woman*—the one who less secure women secretly loathe and admire. Do you ever find yourself in situations where another woman seems to be trying to prove that she's just as good as you, even though the thought of competition never entered your mind? Yep, that's Power Dead-Even Rule at play. Understand it, but refuse to be derailed or dismayed by it when it occurs. It's how some have been nurtured, but is not a reflection of our true nature.

Coming of age in a culture where you are systematically devalued because of your gender, race, or some other inherent characteristic can carry heavy psycho-emotional consequences. Feelings of inferiority are easily triggered when your self-worth is tied to how you compare to someone else. Feelings of envy and jealousy run rampant when you believe that the quality of life you seek is only available in limited quantities and someone else has beaten you to the gate. Left unchecked, this socialized insanity continues to persist. The good news is that we needn't be either a perpetrator or a victim of harmful social norms. We can choose, at this very moment, to live in complete congruence with our highest nature.

As we mature spiritually and accept responsibility for our own healing, we begin to see ourselves and others from a different vantage point. No longer do we operate from archaic platforms of social convention or react mindlessly to people or situations when our own unhealed wounds are triggered. Rather, as wise women, we monitor and manage our thoughts and feelings for any seeds of competition, envy, or jealousy attempting to take root. As soon as we recognize something out of sorts, we remind ourselves of what we know to be true: Competition is vanity. We are each here on a divinely appointed journey.

What's the wise woman's response when witnessing another woman's wonder? She blesses her sister, celebrates her accomplishments, and encourages her forward movement. She sincerely prays for the expansion of her sister's good. She extends this blessing easily because she realizes that any notion of separation between them is pure illusion. As she prays for her sister, she prays for herself. This is why you never have to worry about the miscreant prayers of others directed toward you, because you won't live them out; the heart that authored them will.

The wise woman knows that the good she witnesses in the lives of other women is testimony to what's possible in her own life. The wise woman understands that as she blesses others, she invites the floodgates of goodness to flow unfettered into her own life. A sovereign heart is inspired by the success of others, but an enslaved heart covets and conspires against them, falsely believing that dimming another's light will provide refuge from its own darkness.

There are seven billion of us sharing this earthly journey. We are not here to detract from one another, but to edify and encourage each other's continued unfoldment in this great adventure called *life*. Our entire world is blessed when we grow and blossom together.

MEDITATIVE THOUGHT

I am an expression of the divine presence. I release any spirit of unhealthy comparison or competition and fully embrace the perfection of my unique journey.

WISDOM PROTOCOL

1. ***Identify a situation in your life when you were comparing, coveting, or competing with another woman.*** Use your journal to explore what it was about her—or her life—that left you feeling rattled. Reflect on how you transcended that emotional space.

2. *If this is something you're still working on, spend some time unpacking exactly what she has that you feel is missing for you* (i.e., "People seem to gravitate toward her, and that's something that I'd like to experience"). Being honest with yourself and acknowledging your feelings without judging them frees you to focus on identifying the concrete actions you can take to create the reality you'd like to experience, irrespective of anyone else.

CHAPTER 12

Holding That Racket Kinda Tight, Aren't You?

Sometimes, one must become a master to avoid becoming a slave.

—OCTAVIA BUTLER

Self-awareness is one of the greatest disciplines we can practice. Telling the truth to ourselves, especially when it's *about* ourselves, is right up the wise woman's alley. The ability to stand naked and unafraid in the face of all that you are and all that you have not yet become is liberating. Doing so frees you from the fear of not being enough, or of being too much. You recognize yourself as beautifully human, remaining firmly planted in your trajectory of growth.

For sure, the practice of introspection will bring awareness of your many positive attributes to the fore. You'll be reminded of just how splendid and resilient you already are! It will also shine the spotlight on your *stuff*—those patterns of thought or behavior that are moving a bit more slowly along the evolutionary curve. Most of the time, we are aware of our stuff even when we haven't yet figured out what to do about it. The journey toward purposeful living requires carefully sorting through the internal impediments to our growth. After all, we are not on this journey to become perfect, but to become radically and compassionately honest. Most of all, with ourselves. An excellent place to begin is by exploring the stuff that gets us stuck, then clearing it out.

You know the drill: There's something important you are determined to accomplish. Maybe it's starting a business or moving to a new home. It could be opening yourself up to love again or fulfilling the dream to one day live abroad. Big or small, it's a goal that resonates powerfully within you. Yet despite your best intentions and most sincere efforts, things just don't take flight. On the surface, there are legitimate explanations for persistent inertia. After all, the economy really hasn't been favorable to starting a new business. You almost made an offer on that gorgeous new condo, but you had second thoughts. Being in a committed, loving relationship with your divine-right mate is an earnest desire, but your time on KrazyPeopleMeet.com hasn't turned up any suitable contenders! You feel me? The surface reasons are plausible enough, but deep in your heart, you know that another culprit is at work. And because you're serious about the purpose-filled life seeking its expression through you, that's the very stronghold you are determined to expose and uproot!

I am a recovering perfectionista. Yes, as unreasonable and exhausting as it was, the perfectionism bug had me bogged down. It didn't show up in all areas of my life, but when it did, it was a beast! Sometimes the internal bar I would set for myself was so high that scaling mountain peaks barely seemed enough. Most often, it would show up as taking on too much at one time. My supersized goals weren't impossible to achieve, but my mistake was overcommitting to them. At times it felt like juggling fine china—a completely unnecessary task that left me anxious and tired. The line between *excellence* and *perfection* had become dangerously blurred. It's a tightrope that I've since learned to balance much more carefully. Through prayer and introspection, I began to unpack the behavior and examine the root.

Throughout my life, I've found myself the subject of intense scrutiny. Situations would arise where people, virtually unknown to me, would be knee-deep in my business—trying to figure out what I was doing, who I was doing it with, and how long it had been going on! Being a relatively private person and not prone to forays into other people's business, I found these experiences odd and uncomfortable. It was difficult to fathom why people whom I wasn't particularly curious about would be so curious about me! So being well-prepared became a means of protecting myself against the unwanted glare of outside eyes. This wasn't done to prove anything to anyone else. Rather, it was how I found solace within myself. Once I am confident that I can stand behind my work, the scrutiny of others doesn't bother me. Excellence, I've found, shuts down all manner of covetous noise! When you're bringing your A-game, the results speak for themselves and can withstand scrutiny, undue or otherwise. So, pursuing excellence became my thing, and it has proven to be a tremendous asset.

That said, excellence can be problematic if we obsess over it. In excess, the pursuit of excellence becomes perfectionism. My penchant for perfectionism doesn't happen all the time, or even most of the time; but when it does, I've been known to hold the racket pretty darn tight! I tweak and finesse beyond reason. Check and double-check ad nauseam. I become less decisive, and if left unchecked, I will lock into an indefinite holding pattern until I am convinced that everything is on point. Once I recognized the pattern, I released myself by applying greater discernment in determining when A-game effort was required, and when just showing up was enough. This created lots of wide-open space where there was no pressure to perform and no self-imposed expectations about what my level of performance should be. The joy of the experience became more than enough.

Here's an example. Periodically I enroll in conversational French classes in order to retain functional use of the language. Very often I'm in class with individuals who are multilingual and demonstrate much higher degrees of fluency than my own. And the experience is absolutely delightful! Yes, increasing fluency is important to me, but it's not a stress-worthy goal! I participate in the classes, having conversations with interesting people while flexing my foreign language muscles a little bit. Do others notice that my fluency isn't as high? Maybe. The point is that it really doesn't matter. We're all there for the same reason: to use our language skills in a relaxed and fun environment. I've found a safe landing somewhere between good enough and excellent. How about you?

MEDITATIVE THOUGHT

I am free. Self-mastery frees me from any and all false attachments. Je suis libre!

WISDOM PROTOCOL

1. *Name your racket.* What go-to behavior do you continue to practice even though it doesn't serve you well?
2. *Think about why you're holding that racket so tightly, and explore how your life would be different if you were to loosen your grip.*

SUITE TWO

Restoration

Sometimes you meet yourself on the road before you have a chance to learn the appropriate greeting. Faced with your own possibilities, the hard part is knowing a speech is not required. All you have to say is yes.

—PEARL CLEAGE

#Anew

Dear God,
Who makes all things new
Thanks for including me.
Ashe'.
Amen.
Ameen.

CHAPTER 13

The Isis Factor

I turned myself into myself.

—NIKKI GIOVANNI

One of the most beautiful myths from antiquity is the story of Isis and Osiris. In this Kemetic (Egyptian) archetypal narrative, the goddess Isis is cast as the central character in a tale about life, death, and resurrection. As with all mythology, the story instructs us about the nature of life and the frailties and triumphs of human consciousness. Each character reminds us of the decisions we each make to either ennoble or debase our character with each thought, word, and action. Isis demonstrates the formidable power of love to soothe, heal, and restore. It is precisely when our lives seem broken and scattered that we are called to remember the Isis Factor and energize the power within to be made whole.

There are numerous versions of the myth of Isis and Osiris, and though the details vary across accounts, the central tenets remain consistent. The god Osiris was the beloved ruler of Egypt. He possessed great power and enjoyed tremendous popularity among the people of Egypt. Osiris was married to the supreme goddess Isis, who possessed all of the finer attributes of the lesser goddesses that had come before her. Isis was a formidable leader in her own right who governed alongside her husband and took the helm in his absence. Together Isis and Osiris worked among the people of Egypt to create a harmonious society wherein justice and peace reigned. Egypt flourished under their rule.

Set, the god of disorder, was jealous of his brother Osiris and despised Isis. Brimming with envy, Set devised an elaborate scheme to usurp the throne. When it was announced that Osiris would return from a trip abroad, Set planned an elaborate banquet to celebrate his return. But, in fine frenemy fashion, the celebration was merely a ruse intended to undermine Osiris. During the dinner, Set presented a finely crafted wooden chest and pledged that it would be given to the guest who could fit into it perfectly. Unbeknownst to Osiris, the chest had been designed using his measurements. One by one the guests, who were co-conspirators with Set, attempted to fit into the chest and feigned disappointment about being unable to do so. Finally, Osiris took his turn and fit perfectly. At that moment, the chest was slammed shut and the joints were sealed with lead. The beautiful chest was then cast into the Nile River.

No one told Isis of the demise of her husband, yet her soul knew. Immediately she began to search far and wide for him. After traveling across time and distance, Isis recovered the chest and returned to Egypt with it. Yet, before the Goddess of Magic could properly attend to the remains of Isis's beloved, Set came across the chest himself. Driven by a heart filled with fury, Set opened the chest and chopped the body of Osiris into fourteen pieces, which he then scattered across Egypt. Once again, a deeply grieved Isis set out to recover the remains of her beloved.

Isis crisscrossed Egypt with the precision of a goddess on a mission. One by one she collected the pieces of her husband's body and reassembled them. The fourteenth body part, the phallus, was never found. So, in an act of supreme #BlackGirlMagic, Isis created a golden phallus and then breathed the breath of life into Osiris, bringing him back long enough to conceive a child. Soon after Isis became pregnant, Osiris was able to descend into the underworld, where he became the lord of that domain. Isis gave birth to Horus, the divine son, who would grow to become a great protector of the Egyptian people and ultimately triumph over Set to become Egypt's ruler.

Sisters, there is so much supreme knowledge being shared in this treasured mythological masterpiece. For our purposes, we will focus on the power to resurrect. To what degree have you expressed your power to resurrect the dry-bone situations in your life? Have pieces of your life been ripped apart and tossed into the wind? Or has some deeply cherished aspect of your reality been entrapped and sealed off from the light of day? Perhaps you've found yourself searching, traversing near and far in an attempt to reclaim the sacred entity that has been set adrift. Fret not, beloved! All is not lost. We tap into the Isis Factor when we summon our power to restore. The Isis Factor is the embodiment of the divine feminine attributes that empower us to put together the seemingly disparate pieces of our lives. It is the grace that restores balance. It's the gift that cultivates wholeness.

Restoration is a process that engages the totality of your being. It involves reclaiming dominion of your thoughts, courageously exploring your deepest feelings, and accepting full responsibility for your own wholeness. These are not small feats. Then you must take on the work of determining how to best experience and express that reclaimed wholeness in the world of your affairs. Restoration requires boldly stepping aside from the chambers of familiarity that once governed your existence and establishing new territory for yourself. This newness will encompass every area of your life. As your thoughts and feelings change, so will your choices about how you spend your time and whom you invite into your inner circle. Rather than mindlessly flowing along in the sea of popular opinion, you now apply a higher level of discernment to the affairs of your life. You'll find that even the standards to which you hold yourself are elevated. No longer easily persuaded by the urgings of your human mind, your heart is attuned to the still, small voice within.

You are a woman on a mission. You are squarely about the business of reclaiming and preserving the most cherished parts of your being. You are committed to investing the time and energy needed to resurrect those parts of yourself that have been worn, tattered, and perhaps even beaten by life itself. You are willing, ready, and able to place your stake in solid ground that will nurture and support your transformation into your greater-yet-to-be. Activated by the power of your decision to pursue the fullest expression of your God-intended life, your journey of restoration begins.

As within, so without. When all is well within the inner sanctuary, we are equipped to make a positive difference in the lives of others. We bring the wisdom, patience, and compassion needed to stand as healers and teachers of a new way of life. Until then, our movement and capacity to make a positive impact is constricted by the emotional and spiritual sludge that we haven't yet cleared from our system. Contemplation and activism are twin flames. An open and reflective heart is divinely guided and empowered to express the outworking of a higher truth in the world. Restoration and continuous self-care are essential components of the wise woman's life repertoire.

OUR ROOTS RUN DEEP

Much of what we need to know about personal and communal restoration has already been laid out for us. This knowledge resides in the stories passed down by our foreparents, the messages encoded in our rituals, and the innate wisdom within us. As we take time for contemplative thought, we open ourselves to insights and truths that are as ancient as the DNA that enlivens our cells. How can the rituals and traditions of our ancestors illumine the pathways that we travel today? Their sacred wisdom should not be dismissed or treated as tangential. We must each return home, spiritually and culturally, to realign with wisdom that has sustained humanity since the beginning of time.

As you work your way through this section of the book, think about the wisdom that has been passed down to you. What messages about life have you gleaned from conversations with family or community elders? Is there anything you want to know that would constitute a missing piece of life's puzzle? Our roots run deep with cellular memory and wisdom that we must now summon to facilitate healing on all levels—personal, familial, communal, and global.

Each of the Reflective Essays in this section invites you to focus on an area of your life in which renewal might be needed. Embrace them with a contemplative heart and keep your journal handy to complete the Wisdom Protocols. Record the insights that come to you along the way. As with the preceding chapters, each Reflective Essay is followed by a Meditative Thought (a prompt for meditation, and reflection on the feeling tone it invokes within you) and a Wisdom Protocol (your action plan). Be sure to take time with each component. Your process of transformation is worthy of your full engagement.

CHAPTER 14

Sacred Spaces

Remember, the entrance door to
the sanctuary is inside you.

—RUMI

First I light the candles. Sometimes they stand guard, white and unscented, but more often than not, one or more fragrant candles softly burn. Soon the soothing lemon-basil scent begins to dance around the room as my preparation continues. Next, I select the music. For me, the choice of music is quite fluid; it's a matter of mood. When creating a mellow, contemplative vibe is the goal, *The Gentle Side of John Coltrane* is my go-to companion. If I need a more upbeat, soul-deep energy, I'll set the needle down on an Akua Naru or Laura Mvula album. Then there are those times when the frustrations have mounted higher than my soul feels willing to climb. That's when bumping that Elle Varner anthem is just what's needed to clear the air. "Testimony," performed by Sweet Honey in the Rock, stands out as a perfect-for-any-mood melody.

Next, I check to ensure that my tools are present and easily accessible: journal, pen, books, prayer beads. Right around this time, the kettle whistles, signaling that it's time to prepare a tall cup of ginger-hibiscus tea. It's a homemade brew inspired by an insanely delicious blend once served by the legendary restaurateur Alberta Wright, who was the proprietor of Jezebel restaurant, which was located on 9th Avenue and 45th Street in Manhattan before the elegant jewel closed its doors for good. If you like, you can try my brew:

3–4 cups of water
5–7 thin slices of raw ginger root
¼ cup of dried hibiscus petals
2 cinnamon sticks
Honey or agave nectar, to taste
Juice of ½ lime or lemon (optional)

The tea smells and tastes just like the good side of heaven. As it steeps, I sink into the well-worn comfort of my favorite chair and rest my feet upon her ottoman. This is how I prepare my sacred space.

Every woman should have the luxury of a sacred space to call her own—a place that offers sanctuary from the rest of the world, where her thoughts, dreams, and prayers are free to roam. The creation of sacred spaces, dedicated to contemplation and communion with the Divine, dates back to antiquity. Many of the most spectacular edifices on the planet were designed for this purpose. The Abu Simbel temples in Egypt, the Basilica of San Vitale in Italy, and the Blue Mosque in Turkey immediately come to mind. Their beauty and grandeur are legendary. Just thinking about the vibrational residue of the zillions of prayers offered over many generations, still bouncing off of their walls today, brings chills of wonder. Undoubtedly, these are spiritually powerful places. But so is the prayer bench that your nana knelt on when she and the other church mothers gathered to pray. So is the ground that the indigenous grandmothers stand on when offering invocation. So is the space behind the bathroom door, where last night a woman wept and interceded until she heard the front door open and the steps of her loved one crossing the living room floor. That, too, is holy ground! The most blessed sanctuary I've ever known is located at the foot of my beloved mother's bed. It was there that she read scriptures, sang hymns, offered devotion, provided counsel, and prayed fervently as she kept the high watch over our family. It is through the strength of my beautiful mom's teachings and the consistency of her example that my own spiritual life was seeded and nurtured.

So, you see, your sacred space needn't be massive or ornate. Mine is neither. Rather, it's a cozy area in my bedroom where the chair and ottoman face east, allowing me a clear view of the lake and shoreline. Next to the chair is a small wrought iron accent table where my teacup usually sits, and behind it, a floor lamp. A small, vibrantly colored Moroccan rug warms the floor and helps to mark this area as distinct from the rest of the room. Nearby, there's a console table adorned with candles and fresh cut flowers in varied hues of vibrant colors. Under the console table, a sisal and sweetgrass basket holds my journal, pens, Post-it notes, and highlighters. Opposite the basket sits an array of books. In the colder months, I keep a throw blanket or one of my mom's beautiful handmade quilts nearby. The turntable and music library are located in another area of the room. My sacred space is simple and lovely.

If you don't currently have a designated sacred space, please consider creating one. Your special place should be unique to you. Once you've identified a suitable location within your home, give thought to how you'd like to set it up. Which images and artifacts bring you joy? Include them. Gather your favorite reading materials that invite contemplation and exploration. Decide where to put them. Will you incorporate music, or would a quiet space be more to your liking? Maybe a singing bowl to support your meditation practice would be nice.

Don't feel obligated to buy anything new. Instead, repurpose what you already have. If you choose an area of the house that's easily accessed by others, you'll need to have a conversation with your family about the intended purpose and use of your sacred space. As you begin using this area, you'll notice that the heightened energy will make the space more attractive to others. If you don't establish clear parameters, your sacred space will quickly morph into the new hangout spot for your beloveds. Are you open to nonurgent interruptions when you're in your sacred space? Or do you want to be left alone? Either way, make it plain. Beyond establishing an aesthetically pleasing personal space, there's another benefit that you will quickly realize. Each time that you walk by your space, you will be reminded of the importance of disciplined devotional practice and your role as a spiritual steward of your family. You're not just creating beauty; you're cultivating purpose.

MEDITATIVE THOUGHT

The temple of the Divine is within me.

WISDOM PROTOCOL

Visit Pinterest online or look through magazines to get ideas for creating a beautiful sacred space. Pin or cut out the designs that appeal to you the most. Use them as inspiration as you begin creating a space of your own.

CHAPTER 15

Seeking the Divine

Now like a radiant sky creature
God keeps opening.
God keeps opening
Inside of Me.

—HAFIZ

Sometimes in our eagerness to make a big difference in the outer world, we neglect the proper cultivation of our inner lives. When this happens, we deny ourselves access to the full power of our gifts and talents. Achieving the level of wholeness needed to lead and to serve requires commitment and disciplined self-care. It's difficult to bring one's best contribution to bear when feeling overwrought and depleted. A healthy relationship with Spirit is essential to our well-being. Our inner and outer lives are inseparable. Living a purpose-filled life isn't just about the contributions that we make in the external world; it's also about the women we become, and the character we cultivate along the way.

How do you seek God? What are you doing to cultivate a closer relationship with Spirit? Contrary to popular belief, simply sitting through worship service on the Sabbath and reciting the scriptures from the weekly bulletin isn't enough. Acquiring beautiful prayer beads and placing them on a meticulously crafted prayer altar in your home won't do it either. Nor will punctuating your greetings with holy sounding declarations, such as "Blessed and highly favored!" Though there's absolutely nothing wrong with any of those things, they are not reliable indicators of the strength of your relationship with the Divine.

Outer expressions of devotion aren't necessarily indicative of the true nature of any relationship. We know this is true from our personal lives. If you've ever had someone profess their abiding love for you while repeatedly mistreating you and then chasing their poor behavior with a nice apology gift, you know exactly what I mean. In the end, the carefully crafted words don't matter if your beloved continuously fails to honor the relationship in authentically loving ways.

We expect words and actions to line up. We expect the relationship to be given the time and attention needed to nourish and sustain it. We expect honesty, fidelity, and commitment. When those expectations are not met, we aren't fooled by the glaringly obvious, yet ultimately meaningless, fragments of wounded love that get tossed our way. The same holds true in our relationship with Spirit: The gift without the giver is bare. "Seeking" requires the full engagement of both the heart and mind. It requires the time, focused attention, and discipline needed to build and sustain a meaningful relationship. It requires your active pursuit of knowledge and understanding about the nature of God and how it applies to your life. Seeking can take on many forms. Across faith traditions, however, three pillars routinely appear: prayer, praise, and gratitude.

PRAYER

One of the most precious gifts handed down to me is an 1882 silver dollar. The coin was a gift from a family elder who, around the time I was born, was already nearing the end of her earthly life. It was given to my mother shortly after my birth to hold in trust for me until I was old enough to understand its value and the heartfelt message with which it was passed down. The coin was from Cousin Cecil, a contemporary of my great-grandmother, who wanted me to know that she'd prayed for blessings upon my life while holding the very same silver dollar in her hand.

My mom presented the coin to me on my thirty-first birthday, and I've treasured it ever since. Years later, thinking about the wonder of Cousin Cecil's gift still gives me chills.

I never had the opportunity to meet Cousin Cecil, yet each time I hold the coin in my hand, my heart is filled with awe and gratitude. Not only for Cecil's beneficent prayer offering but also for the presence of mind that led her to leave me a tangible reminder of our spiritual and familial bond. It's such a tremendous gift whenever anyone chooses to go before the altar of the Most High on your behalf. And I don't take it for granted that this beautiful soul and many others have done so for me. Sometimes you just know when you're being lifted by prayers more potent than yours alone. Needless to say, I believe in the power of prayer.

Prayer is the portal through which we commune with the Divine. It is the process by which we align our human will with the will of God. Through the disciplined practice of prayer, a habit of consistent, heartfelt communication with the Divine is cultivated. Through prayer, we intentionally invite Spirit into every aspect of our lives and acknowledge that we are not separate from the source of our creation. Consciously living with an awareness of being in partnership with the Divine emboldens action that is rooted in clarity, confidence, and peace. The more we tap into the sacred wisdom that dwells within, the more open we are to receiving the guidance, insight, and support needed to navigate life successfully. Prayer and contemplation empower us to experience and express life from a higher perspective while protecting us from becoming stymied by the upsets that are common to the human experience. Wherever you are is the perfect place from which to build. We are never outside the love of God. Spirit meets us where we are and grows us from there. An open, honest, and contemplative heart is the most essential tool needed to enliven your prayer practice.

PRAISE

Praise is the heartfelt admiration of an imperfect creation for the works of a perfect creator. When we offer praise, our hearts bow in humility as we honor and celebrate the movement of the Divine in our lives. Praise is the awe felt when witnessing a breathtakingly beautiful sunset, or while resting in the arms of your beloved. Praise is the reverence that rises when hearing the first coo of a newborn child or beholding the last breath as it ascends from the body of a loved one. Praise is the sensation that flutters from head to toe when reflecting on the magnanimity of Spirit and your inextricable connection to all that is. When was the last time that you remember feeling this way?

Expressions of praise are manifold. The vibrations of praise can be felt in djembe patterns, juju rhythms, and conga beats. Seen in the sweeping interpretive movements of liturgical dancers. Heard in Mahalia Jackson's soulful moaning and in the deep bottom of Paul Robeson's voice. Echoed in the harmonies of choirs and chorales. Conveyed by congregants through call and response:

Minister: God is good . . .
Congregation: All the time.
Minister: And, all the time . . .
Congregation: God is good.

Pronouncements of praise are as creative and varied as we are. During Sunday Mass at the Saint John Will I Am Coltrane African Orthodox Church in San Francisco, musicians are encouraged to bring their instruments and join in a jam session featuring the compositions of the mystic and iconic jazz musician John Coltrane. That's right! Live jazz sets are an integral part of how this congregation communicates praise.

Does it surprise you that Trane is considered by many to be a spiritual mystic? It should not. Mystics are ordinary people who experience a transcendence in which the veil between human and spiritual reality is lifted. Mystics ride the high and low tides of life just as we do. They work through their stuff just as we must. As self-knowingness increases, the mystic is able to share bursts of illumined spiritual insights with the world, as Trane did through his music. *A Love Supreme*, released in 1965, is widely regarded as a masterpiece. The album is a four-part movement of praise to the Most High. Definitely check out this album if you don't already have it in heavy rotation. And be sure to read the liner notes! Praise can also be as silent as a sincere thought or as sweet as a pure utterance. "Hallelujah" (Praise the Lord) and "Alhamdulillah" (Praise be to God) are examples from the Christian and Islamic faith traditions.

First and foremost, praise is a condition of the heart that flows from awareness and sincere appreciation of the absolute wonder of the One Life and One Power that expresses through all that is, transcending both the seen and unseen worlds (the world of sense and the world of Spirit). When you have witnessed the magnificent movement of God firsthand, you can't help but praise because your knowledge of the Divine Presence is visceral, not intellectual or philosophical. In the deepest cavern of your soul, you intimately know that the power of the Divine is the realest thing you'll ever experience. How could you *not* be happy about that?

GRATITUDE

If you really want to catapult your life forward, embrace gratitude as a way of life. Being grateful for every good and perfect gift keeps your heart reverent and humble, thereby making your life a magnet for the continued expansion of good. Living from an attitude of gratitude is indicative of your faith in a higher power. It implies your willingness to trust in the ultimate manifestation of goodness, no matter what comes your way. When things go your way, you can say, "Thank you." When things *don't* seem to go your way, you can say, "Thank you." It's not that you're happy to have the challenging situation, but you know that Spirit abides even in the midst of your difficulty. You trust that there will be a secure landing place. You rest in the awareness that you're not alone. So, no matter how uncomfortable the moment feels—"Thank you, God."

Nowhere has the willingness to embrace the practice of gratitude and summon its power been more beautifully demonstrated than by the participants in a series of Sacred Circle sessions that I facilitated at a transitional program. The group was composed of women who were nearing the completion of their prison terms, and who were living in transitional housing as they prepared to re-enter the community. Their stories and reasons for being there were as varied as their faces. Yet they each shared the pain of having been separated from loved ones and a sense of uncertainty about the future that awaited them. Each week our group would gather in a large multipurpose room, our chairs placed in a wide circle. A distinct theme served as the focal point for each gathering. We explored issues of love, loss, learning to love again, restitution and forgiveness, effective co-parenting, and a host of other topics. Each woman kept a journal in which she would write insights and observations as they occurred to her throughout the week. Our conversations were rich and heartfelt!

There's something about going through the fiery furnace of adversity that strips away the need for pretense. The stakes were high! These women were about the business of rebuilding lives, so there was no room for superficiality or timidity of thought. When you're hungry for healing, you bring your whole self to the process. At the end of our circle time, we would close out by having each woman share something for which she was grateful. There was never an instance when someone had nothing to share. Some of these women had lived through pure hell and endured horrors too awful to write about, yet each and every one of them was able to find some kernel of goodness for which they were thankful. Even as the shadow of incarceration lurked behind them and uncertainty hovered ahead, they recognized the light of the Divine within their daily experiences. We are each challenged to do the same. Who or what are you grateful for in this moment? Decide how you will express the appreciation that you feel. Resist the temptation to send a quick email or text message. Dig deeper and make your words really count. Consider an in-person visit to share your sentiments face-to-face. Or, take the time to write a heartfelt letter to communicate your gratitude.

MEDITATIVE THOUGHT

Through the disciplined practice of prayer, praise, and gratitude, my life is restored.

WISDOM PROTOCOL

Is there an area of your devotional practice that you would like to develop more fully? If so, which pillar must you cultivate? Determine three actions that you will take within the next week to begin fostering a deeper inner connection. What is it that keeps you from playing fully in this area of your life? Naming the impediment is the first step toward reclaiming your power.

CHAPTER 16

Who's Guarding Your Heart?

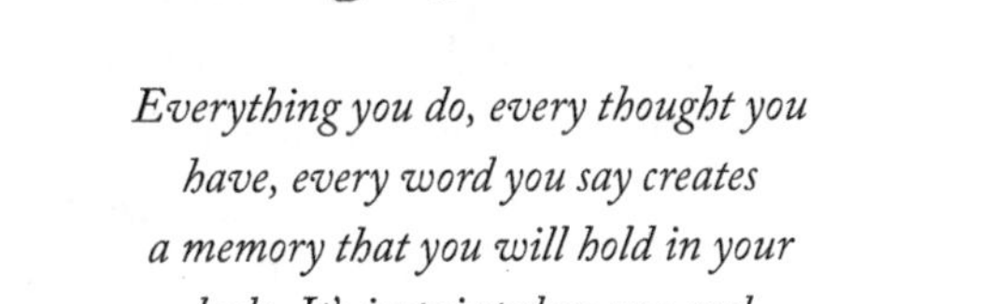

Everything you do, every thought you have, every word you say creates a memory that you will hold in your body. It's imprinted on you and affects you in subtle ways—ways you are not always aware of. With that in mind, be very conscious and selective.

—PHYLICIA RASHAD

How carefully do you guard your heart? This is a duty that none of us can afford to take for granted. The word *heart* in this instance is actually a scriptural reference that carries a much broader meaning. Proverbs 4:23 reads, "Keep and guard your heart with all vigilance and above all that you guard, for out of it flow the springs of life." *Heart* refers to the accumulated thoughts and feelings that penetrate our innermost being. This scripture is cautioning us to be careful about what we allow to take root inside of us because those emotions and habits of mind will call forth their equivalents into the world of our affairs. Life is a dance of choices and consequences; whether your particular two-step is rhythmic and graceful or offbeat and awkward depends on the thoughts and feelings that guide the movement of your consciousness.

Our experiences, or *springs of life*, are the result of what we're holding in heart, even when we are not consciously aware of what we've allowed to take residence deep within. Look around: The effects of this truth are at work and clearly evident. Have you ever known someone who was addicted to watching late-night news even though doing so filled her with so much fear that she was hesitant to leave the house in the mornings? Yet, like clockwork, she tuned in faithfully each evening to get refills of the words and images that robbed her of sleep at night and haunted her waking hours. It wasn't her conscious intention to become afraid, but she confirmed and reinforced her fearful beliefs every time she tuned in. In time, her efforts became fruitful as she actually became a prisoner to her own thoughts. She lived out the unspoken credo of her life—"Danger is imminent!"—even when the reality of her outer world posed no immediate threat.

Left to its own devices, an idle mind can take some interesting and ultimately painful excursions. In this instance, "idle" refers to unguarded mental activity. Consider the wife who faithfully watches *Cheaters*—a reality show in which accusations of infidelity are investigated and exposed—as her mindless, midday television indulgence. Pretty harmless, right? Only until the constant barrage of episodes about dishonest spouses causes her to wonder about the level of fidelity in her own marriage. At first she easily dismisses these musings, but soon the rogue thoughts have more grit and staying power. She can't explain why, but feelings of distrust for her husband begin to mount. Even though there are no "signs" of cheating, she can't shake the thought that it *might* be happening. One day her suspicions get the best of her, and she decides to confront her husband. An argument ensues. She accuses. He denies. They're both hurt and heated. They both say things that would have been better left unsaid. Bingo! Anger, hurt, and turmoil were called forth, and they answered. That night she falls across the bed, exhausted from the emotional drain of having finally met her creation face-to-face, still unaware of the role she played in what sprang forth.

Thankfully, the wise woman sojourner is too astute to remain stuck in old, useless habits. A significant part of the restoration process involves being mindful enough to surround yourself with people, places, and ideas that enliven you and support you in being your best self. Become a practitioner of what I refer to as "Vibe-ology," the practice of pausing to study how you feel when interacting with external or internal stimuli. Begin by simply paying attention to how people, environments, and even your own thoughts affect you. What energy, or vibe, are you picking up? Notice how the stimuli register emotionally. Ask yourself, *How am I feeling?* and *Why do I feel this way?* Make note of your observations as patterns begin to emerge. Try not to judge what comes up, and resist the temptation to make others responsible for the emotional charge that you are experiencing. There will be some instances where you're legitimately picking up on energies emanating from an external source. But, there will also be times when what you're feeling is the outward projection of an internal trigger—a fear or insecurity perhaps—that's been activated. By slowing down and checking in with yourself, you become more self-aware and create the space to recalibrate as needed.

Who do you call when you need invigorating conversation? What are you doing when the time just seems to fly by and you find yourself immersed in deep laughter? When you need emotional support, who's on speed dial to stand and agree with you? Where do you go when you seek renewal? Your favorite park, the home of a friend, the local music store, or a day spa? Explore which of the infinite choices works best for you. Pay attention to what brings you joy, and intentionally invite more of it into your life. You are worthy of relationships and experiences that honor and reflect back to you the true beauty of who you are.

Here's the key: We're constantly taking in elements from the social, emotional, and physical environments that surround us. It's up to us to ensure that what we're allowing into our atmosphere supports us on the journey toward more purposeful living. Over time, if we fail to do so, we become spiritually emaciated from years of not being valued, acknowledged, and supported in ways that nourish our souls. Sistah-friend, guard your sacred chamber. And be vigilant about it!

MEDITATIVE THOUGHT

As I guard my heart, my mind, body, and spirit are restored.

WISDOM PROTOCOL

Identify one restorative practice that would contribute to your spiritual growth. Maybe it's joining a meditation circle or enrolling in a dance or quilting class. It can be anything that brings you greater peace and joy. Then, incorporate the new restorative practice into your life within the next thirty days.

CHAPTER 17

Reclaiming Ritual

Rituals are the formulas by which harmony is restored.

—TERRY TEMPEST WILLIAMS

The day of the wedding was bright but crisp. I remember being glad that the sun was shining because I didn't want my pretty new dress or shiny new shoes to get wet. My mom had pressed my hair to perfection the night before. A neatly trimmed and softly curled bang kissed my forehead. The back had been swept into a small, knotted bun. Yes, an updo was wedding appropriate. After bathing and drying off, I smoothed the homemade mixture of lotion and olive oil over my body and rubbed it in. My smooth cocoa-colored skin gleamed like new money. Mom wiped off the excess shine and helped me get dressed, even spraying me with a couple of squirts of her grown lady perfume to mark the occasion. Once ready, we piled into my father's car and headed to King David Baptist Church. The excitement and nervousness gave me butterflies. This was my first time being in a wedding. I was seven years old. The bride was ten.

The annual Tom Thumb wedding was a favorite program at our family church. The mock wedding was sponsored by the youth department. After weeks of practice, the bride and groom, bridesmaids and groomsmen, flower girl and ring bearer would take their positions and wait for the processional to begin. The ceremony proceeded with the same structure and formalities that would be performed during an adult wedding. The presence of the community to bear witness. The seating of the family. The processional of the bridesmaids. The bride's entrance. Giving away the bride. The exchange of vows. There was no kiss, but a light hug and the awkward staring of two ten-year-olds who'd just been pronounced *man* and *wife*. A cake and punch reception followed. There were no gifts.

Major life events such as marriage, death, and the birth of a child are marked by ceremony and ritual in cultures across the globe. Rituals are the conduit through which the norms, values, and beliefs of a culture are communicated, reinforced, and preserved. Rituals may be culturally unique, but they are universally practiced. Rituals aren't mysterious, though many embody mystical elements. They are not spooky, though they are sometimes misunderstood by those to whom they are unfamiliar. Every time you've placed candles on a birthday cake, lit them, and asked someone to blow them out while making a wish, you were participating in a ritual. To someone unfamiliar with the practice and observing it for the first time, it may seem a bit odd. But you're not engaging in any underworld, Illuminati activity. Of course not! You're simply engaging in the practice of ritual to honor the occasion as a moment of significance.

Rituals center the mind and assist those gathered in holding a common intention. The collective consciousness of a people or community is expressed through its practice of ritual. Cultural identity is shaped and strengthened through the acknowledgment and repetition of practices that represent shared ideals. In traditional African societies, and historically in African-American communities, marriage was conceptualized as an institution of importance to the community as a whole. Through this worldview, marriage held significant meaning and purpose as a channel for the spiritual and intimate union of the couple, the coming together of two families, the nurturing and raising of children, and the sustainment of strong communities. Marriage was held as aspirational, protective, and a means of demonstrating the virtue of being responsible to and for someone other than oneself. Indeed, in the African-American tradition, Tom Thumb weddings were conceptually much more than a cute program for children. The ceremony was one of socio-cultural seed planting, designed to foster expectations and help shape visions of the future. Cultural continuity cannot be preserved in the absence of ritual. When we abandon ritual, we relinquish the bind that has held us together across the deep waters of time. When considering the role of marriage and family, where do we take our cues from today?

You may have grown up, as I did, in a community where two-parent households were the norm. Both mother and father were present in almost every home on the block. There were few single-parent households, though they did exist. There were also households without children, though they, too, were the exception. The neighborhood where I grew up was fairly typical of working- and middle-class Black communities in the 1970s. Marriage rates in the Black community remained relatively stable from Reconstruction in the late 1800s through the 1970s. That's pretty remarkable considering the formidable odds our families have faced over time. Even during their enslavement, when Black marriages were not legally allowed, our foreparents married by establishing unions that were sanctioned by the Creator and held as sacred by the community. They created rituals, like jumping the broom, to have the community bear witness as two became one. Following emancipation, obtaining legal status for marriages initiated during slavery and reuniting with family members from whom they had been separated were among the most frequently requested forms of assistance from the Freedmen's Bureau, the government agency established to assist formerly enslaved persons transitioning to emancipated life.

It wasn't until the 1980s that an alarmingly sharp increase in the number of Black women who never married was first noted. This spike correlates highly with the increased incarceration rates of Black men resulting from the failed War on Drugs, which was launched around the same time. Today, many young people have never lived in communities where healthy models of marital relationships exist. Often the most powerful models for healthy partnerships and parenting relationships that they are exposed to come from television shows—fictional accounts of a reality they have never personally known. It's estimated that as many as 72 percent of Black children are raised in a single-parent household, a percentage much higher than the 26 percent average for the U.S. as a whole. Shifts in cultural views about marriage and changing attitudes about single parenthood are among the factors contributing to these numbers. As always, we must ask what these numbers really mean for us.

Sometimes the institution of marriage gets a bad rap for bestowing undue privilege upon men at the expense of women. We've each witnessed or experienced instances where this was true. However, when this imbalance occurs, the problem is that the norms of patriarchy are dictating how the marriage functions. It's been that way in far too many instances, but it doesn't have to be that way at all. The institution of marriage, itself, is neutral. Each couple is empowered to construct their union in any way that they please. Marriage can be an oppressive cavern or an illuminating incubator for growth and support. Marriage is whatever the parties involved construct it to be.

One of the most prominent and culturally proliferated stereotypes is that of the "strong black woman." The problem isn't that Black women aren't strong. We most certainly are. The problem is that the stereotype is a partial truth that fails to speak to the totality of who we are. The "strong black woman" cultural archetype ignores the nurturance and support that Black women need in order to thrive. Overreliance on this stereotype has resulted in unrealistic expectations being imposed upon us. We've been talking about it for generations. The esteemed author Zora Neale Hurston called it out perfectly in her classic 1937 novel, *Their Eyes Were Watching God.* Speaking through her "everywoman" heroine Janie Crawford she proclaims, "De nigger woman is de mule uh de world so fur as Ah can see." It's disheartening to think about how much truth those words still carry today.

Stereotypes, when internalized, shape how we see ourselves. Overidentification with the "strong black woman" stereotype has resulted in far too many of us taking on more than any healthy person should. And we often increase that burden by feeling inadequate when we fail to do, be and have it all. Being everything to everybody, at the expense of ourselves, has worn the fabric of our spiritual, emotional, and physical well-being very thin. A review of health and other quality of life indicators reveal that far too many of us perpetually exist on the brink of breakdown.

The morbidity rates for Black women are higher for numerous illnesses, including hypertension, diabetes, and stroke, among others. According to the American Heart Association, over 49 percent of Black women aged twenty and older have heart disease. This means that half of us are fighting an uphill battle with our health right out of the gate. Enough already. Yes, it is true that these ailments are directly linked to nutritional deficiencies and dietary excesses. We must raise the bar on the choices that we are making in those areas. Simultaneously, we must also explore the other areas of our lives that remain undernourished and unsatiated. True restoration requires whole-woman solutions. What's your take on the relationship between the higher rates of morbidity and mortality experienced by Black women and the disproportionate levels of responsibility that we often shoulder alone?

Let's circle back to our discourse on the institution of marriage. Strong marriages and families have long been the bedrock of communities of color. Against the most daunting odds, our families have fought to survive—demonstrating extraordinary resilience while enduring systemic destabilizations that have persisted for generations. Without a doubt, the enduring strength and sacrifice of Black women has been key to our collective survival, as has the sacrifice and strength of Black men. Strength, however, must be measured by more than our ability to get things done by ourselves. Why aren't we talking about how hard it is to go it alone? What if we expand the definition of strength to include the formation of loving, healthy, and committed partnerships? What if we conceptualized vulnerability as an attribute of strength? What if we committed to unlearning the narrative that keeps us separate and alone, embracing instead the lessons of unity and resiliency passed down to us by our foreparents? Who, then, would we become?

We must challenge the programming that causes us to shy away from the possibilities and complexities inherent in building and sustaining healthy, loving relationships with Black men. Fannie Lou Hamer once stated, "You know I'm not hung up on this liberating myself from the 'black' man—I'm not going to try that thing." Here's what her words mean to me. We don't want to be free *from* Black men, we want to be free *with* them. Free to construct marriages that are equal partnerships, rooted in love, respect, and reciprocity. Free to experience and express intimacy that sustains us emotionally, mentally, sensually, and spiritually. Free to support each other in fulfilling our respective aspirations of self-actualization. Free to build families, communities, and institutions that affirm and strengthen who we are individually and collectively. And free to create sanctuary that buffers us from the attacks on psychologically healthy selfhood that we endure *together*. What do the words of Fannie Lou Hamer mean to you? Is marriage still aspirational for contemporary women? What about you? Is marriage something that you personally desire?

MEDITATIVE THOUGHT

Embracing culture restores life. I am a proud conduit of the culture.

WISDOM PROTOCOL

Examine your thoughts about marriage. Is the institution of marriage still relevant? Take a sheet of paper and fold it in half vertically. Label the left side *Pros* and the right side *Cons*. Then list what you consider to be the pros and cons of marital relationships in the twenty-first century. Describe how the ideal modern-day marriage would look and work. Initiate a conversation with women and men whose perspectives you value about the role of marriage in personal and community life. Ask the question: *Should marriage be restored as a cultural value?*

CHAPTER 18

Practicing Patience

Patience is the companion of wisdom.

—ST. AUGUSTINE

Are you patient and slow to offend? Can you overlook minor missteps without letting them ruffle your feathers? Truthfully, I'm much better at this on some days than on others. When I'm firmly grounded in my spiritual practice, I'm better able to brush off the actions of others that I perceive as insensitive or offensive. But when I'm caught off guard because I haven't afforded myself the level of self-care necessary, my patience can wear really thin. Sometimes this results in words, actions, or attitudes that I later regret. This doesn't happen often, but I'm not immune. What about you? Have you noticed any patterns of impatience? The good thing about understanding our personal patterns is that it allows us to intervene more quickly when we first feel things going awry.

Our patience can be challenged in any number of ways. It doesn't take much to get most people out of sorts. To be reminded of just how quickly impatience arises, the next time you're out and about, observe drivers in rush hour traffic. It's amazing how many people get really, really ticked off with other drivers over minor infractions. What an awful way to begin or end the day! If it's not the driver in the next car, maybe it's the colleague who's always late for meetings. The nosey neighbor. Or, the friend who calls several times a day, every day, with little consideration of your time. One thing is certain. Life serves up plenty of opportunities for us practice patience. It's up to us to accept the challenge.

Sometimes we become impatient, not because of what someone has done, but because they hold beliefs that differ fundamentally from those we hold dear. Be honest. How many times have you listened to someone express a different political or religious point-of-view and found yourself secretly proclaiming them to be the most ill-informed person on the planet? You're on one side of the room thinking, *How can anyone be so unenlightened?* And they're on the other side of the room wondering, *How has the species survived with people who think that way?* In that very moment, if a conscious decision to practice patience is not brought to bear, the willingness to listen is subsumed by the need to be right. What might have been an interesting and informative exchange of ideas becomes a battle of wills, in which no one wins.

These minor upsets have a cumulative effect over time. Left unchecked, their impact mounts. Before long, it seems that almost everybody is doing something to stomp on that last, good nerve we've been trying so hard to preserve. Once we've had all that we can take, we become a bundle of disheveled, reactionary energy lying in wait for the next person who dares to cross us. And, there's the rub. Each time that we allow our mental and emotional energies to be usurped in this manner, we do ourselves a disservice. We're the ones who end up emotionally and mentally depleted, while the world around us continues to spin with vigor.

LEILANI'S STORY

There are those seasons when our impatience isn't with other people at all, but with God. Perhaps a prayer wasn't answered in the manner hoped for, or within the desired timeframe. Maybe some long-held yearning remains unfulfilled, leaving us to wonder if our prayers are still getting through. We pray, *Hello, God, are you there?* Or maybe life ushers in some situation that stretches us beyond what we think we can bear. We experience doubt and become impatient whenever we feel we've become disconnected from the Divine.

This is precisely how Leilani and Nabil felt when their four-year-old son, Sabri, was first diagnosed with autism. As parents, they held a high vision of a happy, healthy, and vibrant life for all three of their children. They were knocked off-center when it was confirmed that the pathway would be much more arduous for their youngest son. Living with such a complex disorder has, at times, proven to be overwhelming for the family. Leilani acknowledges that caring for her son has demanded that she cultivate levels of patience beyond anything that she knew existed. She notes, however, that the journey has also brought tremendous gifts. Leilani shares:

> *There was so much that I took for granted before. Our lives were fast-paced and filled with the constant rush of activity. But Sabri's presence has required that we slow down significantly in order to understand his needs. Watching our son struggle to complete even the most basic activities of life has been incredibly humbling. Early on, I was crushed each time that he would pull away from me when I would reach out to hug him. And, I'll admit it. I didn't always demonstrate the most excellent patience. I was pained and frustrated. Many nights, I cried myself to sleep after long days of feeling like nothing we did for Sabri was enough. The breakthroughs that we so desperately sought were not easily achieved or fast coming.*

Leilani and Nabil's marriage was also challenged. The emotional and economic toll of having a child with autism created tensions and resentments between the couple, who increasingly became impatient with one another. "Some days we were so short with each other that it was difficult to remember that we'd once been great friends and partners. There was a period of time when I wasn't even happy to see my husband walk through the door. I felt angry and alone, even though I could see that he was struggling just like I was. Nothing felt like enough."

Leilani credits a series of counseling sessions with their Imam as the beginning of the turnaround for their marriage, saying:

> *The counseling sessions created a safe space for us to share our fears and frustrations while reconnecting to the deep love that we share. Through this challenging experience, we have both grown more patience with ourselves and one another. We are allowing this journey to mold us into better people, partners, and parents. Better days are ahead, and we trust that Allah will not put upon us any more than we can bear. We will be fine, all of us, together.*

Leilani continued by reflecting on how practicing patience has benefitted her. "I look back and laugh at how fragile my peace was before Sabri was born. Having to focus on what really matters makes it so easy to let go of the petty annoyances that pop up during the day. I'm not nearly as easily rattled as I used to be when things don't go my way. As my patience has blossomed, my peace of mind has been restored."

Patience is a skill cultivated through disciplined practice. Begin by reflecting on why you are motivated to become more patient. Are you seeking to improve a relationship? Or, perhaps, to decrease stress? Whatever your motivation is, remind yourself of the benefits derived from your quest to be more patient and set a demonstrative goal that you can measure your progress against. Practicing patience is restorative because it requires that we operate outside of the comfort zones that appease our egoic minds. We transcend the boundaries of how we would prefer things to be and surrender to the perfect outworking of the Divine. As with any other attribute that we nurture over time, patience becomes our nature as we continue to apply it. Understanding that patience enables the fulfillment of purpose, we endeavor to remain conscious enough at all times to make the best Spirit-inspired decisions about how to respond to whatever life brings. When we've invested in disciplined self-care, we're not as easily thrown off-kilter by challenging situations or the actions of others. Instead, we are drawn to go within and discern right action before making any outward moves. By taking care of ourselves and consistently engaging in the practices that keep us grounded, we cultivate a deeper wellspring from which to draw upon when needed.

Allow patience, kindness, compassion, and other virtues needed for daily living to take root within you! Nurture the attributes of Spirit that you wish to experience in your everyday life by applying them whenever an opportunity arises. So, the next time that someone does something to tick you off, be slow to offend—very, very slow to offend—until, at last, you cast off offense entirely and allow patience to prevail.

MEDITATIVE THOUGHT

As I practice patience, my peace of mind is restored.

WISDOM PROTOCOL

Know yourself and grow yourself. Identify the emotional triggers that are most challenging for you. What is it that most easily takes you off center? What new thoughts or behaviors must you embrace in order to demonstrate greater patience when these triggers are pulled?

CHAPTER 19

Embracing Oneness

I look at an ant and I see myself.

—MIRIAM MAKEBA

Several years ago, Senegalese musical icon and cultural activist Youssou N'Dour and Swedish-born singer Neneh Cherry composed and recorded an internationally chart-topping duet entitled "7 Seconds." The song's trilingual lyrics reflect on the problem-free innocence that children experience when they are first born. We each enter this life unfettered by notions of lack, limitation, violence, and separation. But all too soon, after about seven seconds, the voices of the new world rush in to shape us. From that point on, someone somewhere is trying to tell us what and how to think, who to love and when to hate, and where to go to become a reality TV superstar. The song resonates with many because it's such a poignant reminder that human discord is the result of how we're nurtured and is not our inherent nature. Our belief in the inevitability of poverty, the permanence of war, and our separation—one from the other—are all mental constructs that play themselves out as our collective reality. When we become courageous enough to change the thought narrative, we will indeed change the world.

Most people live fairly insular lives, finding themselves surrounded by people who are pretty much just like them. This is especially true when we examine the parameters with which we establish emotional proximity to others. To some degree, we all seek the comfort of familiarity, and that isn't a bad thing. We connect around shared values and visions of life. We cling to the kindred spirit that permeates places where our names are easily pronounced and the aromas of our foods remain sweetly familiar. It's within the sanctuary of the familiar that the continuity of our cultural identity is preserved and the teachings of our ancestors are passed on. On this hallowed and steady ground, we feel most honored and accepted. Familiarity can be beautiful and has its merits.

Our tendency to huddle in the sanctuary of the familiar only becomes problematic when we never venture out to explore and interact with the people and places existing outside of what's already known to us. In the absence of meaningful connections with those who are significantly different from us, we are left to rely on sound bites and stereotypes to inform our understanding of others. It's within the murky waters of separation that distrust, disdain, and even hatred are bred. Think about it: Have you ever met people who harbor disdain for people from another part of the world, even though they've rarely, if ever, visited that place and don't personally know anyone who claims the distant and disparaged land as home?

Where the mind goes, the heart soon follows. Once the idea that others are distinctly different from you takes root, it becomes easy to dehumanize them, effortless to believe the worst about them, and comforting to fantasize about being better than they are. Traveling on a thought trajectory rooted in separation obscures the reality that your well-being is inextricably linked to that of those you've dismissed as being "the other." Embracing oneness isn't about losing your identity; it's about expanding your notion of who you are until you recognize that your heart is big enough to let others in. When we come together and commune with those who have had different life experiences, our own worldview is broadened and transformed. Misconceptions are clarified, and irrational fears are inoculated. Intentionally creating opportunities to learn from one another and grow together is essential to our spiritual and social evolution. Having been the beneficiary of these types of gatherings, I can attest to their power.

The African Friendship Society was an informal gathering that brought together people from across the diaspora for cultural exchange and fellowship. The group was comprised of professionals, graduate students, professors, and everyday folk who were open to the experience. We met in the home of Sister Luvenia, a healer and cherished member of the cultural community. Before crossing the threshold of the front door, the aromas of groundnut stew or jollof rice would come outside to greet you. They were accompanied by the pulsating beat of musical rhythms that crossed the global expanse. The sounds of Fela, Makeba, Marley, and Cruz filled the air. Once inside, it was as if you'd been invited to a Pan-African Congress after-glow. We debated global politics and the challenges faced by Black liberation movements. We discussed history and art. We celebrated birthdays, graduations, and the formation of new families. And, we *daaanced* as if life itself depended upon the strength of our wind and the movement of our feet. These monthly gatherings were effectually human interaction labs wherein we were able to experience ourselves and one another within a broader, global context. It was a forum where we could be enriched by the differences that existed between us and simultaneously strengthened by our common bonds.

Since the nights of the African Friendship Society, I've been blessed with the opportunity to travel broadly and establish bonds of friendship with amazing people around the world. What I've learned along the way is that at the core we all seek the same things. We desire to love and be loved well. We crave a sense of belonging and a meaningful connection to others. We seek peace of mind and more than fleeting moments of happiness. We hope for a full measure of good health. We want to live lives that matter. We yearn to fulfill purpose. And we exist to help one another bring these aspirations to fruition.

Much of the bigotry and fear that keeps some people stuck is due to a lack of exposure. People who live in small worlds are prone to thinking small thoughts. My earliest curiosities about other people, places and cultures were stoked by my parents who planned family trips each summer. Our vacation travels were instrumental in helping me to develop a sense of place that extended beyond my immediate surroundings. There's something empowering about experiencing the "other" that reinforces the sense of self – the awareness that you can hold your own anywhere and with anyone. There are an infinite number of ways to expand the parameters of your existing world. Invite new experiences often. Allow your intrinsic curiosity to take you to new places, where you will interact with different people. It could be a neighborhood across town or a community across the ocean. Just explore!

Sometimes I'll get together with a couple of friends and go road-tripping. We'll drive to cities within a few hours' distance, just to experience something new. We've had all types of amazing adventures, from witnessing the birth of a calf (bowing in respect to heifers everywhere) to crashing a Hindi wedding reception. No, I don't regularly crash receptions, but in this instance, the beat of the music was so sick that it couldn't be helped! (The DJ was mixing "Beware of the Boys" by Panjabi MC and "My Name Is Sheila.") Plus, the hosts were super gracious and warmly welcomed us to join in the fun. Road-tripping is something you might consider incorporating into your routine. There are all manner of delights and wonders awaiting discovery along the highways and byways near you.

Go and see the world. There's a beautiful, friendly world out there awaiting you! I've been fortunate to travel to quite a few places and, with God's grace, I'll get to experience many more. Everywhere that I've set foot warm and friendly people have met me. Sure, different cultures express their personas in unique ways, but that's all part of the magic. With the right planning, international travel can be cost-effective too. Check the airlines to see which discounts or vacation specials are being offered. Identify events or points of interest in other places and plan a trip around them. The exhibition *Basquiat: Boom for Real* at the Schirn in Frankfurt and a visit to the Mémorial ACTe on the French Caribbean island of Guadeloupe are examples of such trips that are on my short list. The former is a landmark art exhibition featuring the works of the iconic, Brooklyn-born artist Jean-Michel Basquiat. The latter is a cultural center that is part of UNESCO's Slave Route Project, a global initiative to promote rapprochement—the building or restoration of harmonious relations between peoples connected by the tragic and shared legacy of the transatlantic slave trade. Both provide great opportunities to explore the world just a little bit more.

If getting out of the city or country isn't doable right now, find other ways to invite the world in. Reading, a favorite pastime that was introduced to me by my mother during my childhood, is a wonderful way to expand one's knowledge of different people and places. The experience of wandering through and engaging new worlds via the written word is incredibly addictive. Arundhati Roy, Edwidge Danticat, Chimamanda Ngozi Adichie, Colin Channer, Dreda Say Mitchell, and Dinaw Mengestu are among the writers whose works have welcomed me into new worlds. Naguib Mahfouz, Mariama Ba, Yiyun Li, Zadie Smith, Alejandro Zambra, and countless other magnificent writers have done the same. The wonders of the written word beckon us to expand our horizons. Think about someplace in the world that sparks your curiosity, then visit a local library or bookstore to find books that will help you learn about that location.

The final tip I'll offer is to explore the world through independent and foreign films. I first began watching art house films when I was sixteen, and a university freshman. Some days, rather than hanging out in the student union when there was a significant break between classes, I'd go to the library or visit a department on campus where screenings were being hosted. Watching independent and experimental films continues to bring me joy. Many excellent films will never receive mainstream distribution, despite being intelligently and artfully done. You'll get over reading the subtitles fairly quickly. That part will feel like second nature before long. What will really captivate you is how different the structure and cadence of the films are from what is typically presented in Hollywood-produced movies. It's an entirely different experience and one that I hope you'll come to enjoy.

We are citizens of the global community. There are good people all over the earth's expanse waiting to befriend you. Don't keep them waiting. Get out there and experience the wonder, near and far, that surrounds you. Do so, and I promise that your life will be forever changed. Hey, let's take a selfie when we meet at the airport!

MEDITATIVE THOUGHT

I am an ambassador of the beloved community.
I am a citizen of the world.

WISDOM PROTOCOL

Break the pattern of insularity in your life. Create experiences that put you in direct contact with those who are different from you in some significant way. Intentionally seek to build purposeful relationships that restore your awareness of your connectedness to all that is. Journal about your experience and its impact on your life.

CHAPTER 20

Kindred: Reigniting the Spirit of Community

With all things and in all things, we are relatives.

—SIOUX PROVERB

Humans are meant to live in community—but what does that really mean? The term "community" is bandied about so often that its meaning has become obscured. For many, it's merely a term of convenience that describes how they're willing to relate to you when times are good and the stakes aren't too high. For others, it's the number of *Facebook Friends* who regularly respond to their postings. Being in authentic community can't be solely defined by factors such as physical or social proximity, DNA, adherence to shared political, cultural, or religious beliefs, or by membership in the same organization. It's true that we often create community with those who share some meaningful connection to our lives, but common bonds are rarely in and of themselves sufficient to produce the type of authentic community we're discussing here.

Authentic communities are safe spaces where both formation and affirmation occur. The shaping and refining of individual selfhood is facilitated by the support and encouragement of the collective. Within these incubators of growth, there is a sacred agreement between members to invest in and support the unfoldment of the highest form of self-expression for each individual and the group. A fierce and fearless love serves as the foundation upon which the building blocks of authentic community are built: connection, character, courage, and commitment. In traditional African cosmology, the community is the vehicle through which individual identity emerges and is shaped. *I am because we are, and since we are, therefore I am.* Who you ultimately become is invariably influenced by those who surround you. Are you surrounded by people who genuinely support you in achieving the fullest possible expression of your purpose? If so, bless yourself by reciprocating and fully immersing yourself in that community! If not, it's time to seek more fertile ground.

There are different levels of relationship within the broader construct of community. The majority of people who live in your neighborhood, work at your job, and worship on adjoining pews are not on your "go-to" list when you need help managing the highs and lows of life. Sometimes members of your own family aren't on the "go-to list." It's sweet when it happens, but even bloodlines offer no guarantee that the levels of intimacy, trust and vulnerability required to be in authentic community will be present. Relationships on the micro, or personal level, are reserved for those with whom you share a high degree of socio-emotional closeness. It is within the sanctuary of this intimate circle that the unfoldment of your life, with all of the inevitable twists and turns, is affirmed and supported. This core group is called by many names: besties, bffs, tribe, family, close friends, squad, and crew. No matter what you call them, you know who they are; you know that you can count on them and you treasure their presence in your life. This intimate circle is key to restoration.

On the macro level, there exists the collective community which is broader in scope and vital to advancing shared goals that contribute to the betterment of the whole. Membership in the collective community is organized around a central unifying element (i.e., race, gender, country of origin) and the recognition of common interests. When references are made to the Black community, the Women's Movement, and immigrant enclaves, for example, it is this broader context of the collective community that is being addressed. Identification with the collective community is usually involuntary. One is born into the Hispanic community, the Jewish community, or the middle class, for instance. Yet affiliation with the community is most certainly a matter of choice. We each decide whether or not to support the joint interests shared by our collective community kinfolk.

When properly organized and galvanized, the power of community cannot be denied. The firm, unified efforts of the community have brought down systems of injustice and forged pathways to greater equity across the globe, from Montgomery to Johannesburg and at innumerable points in between. Somberly, we have also witnessed what can happen when the power of community is usurped and exploited—relegating once-vital and influential communities to little more than reliable pawns who demand little while giving far too much. Let's explore the building blocks of authentic communities that are the source of their strength.

CONNECTION

Connection is fostered by a sense of belonging. It's the awareness of being an integral part of something more significant than the individual self. A deep and shared knowing that the life and well-being of each member matters to the others is the heartbeat of an authentic community. Here there is no ambiguity about the importance of your life and your right to fully express the gifts and talents within you. Indeed, it is within the context of the authentic community that these attributes are enthusiastically called forth, nurtured, and celebrated. A sense of belonging emerges where safe spaces exist—where we experience emotional safety and the freedom to simply be, forming a web of relationships wherein our strengths are met with appreciation, and our fragilities are greeted with compassion.

CHARACTER

Just as the strength of individual character can be measured by the degree to which certain virtues or vices are demonstrated, so can the characterological makeup of a community. This isn't an entirely foreign concept. There was a time within the Black community when certain types of crimes would be reported on the evening news, and a collective cry of relief—declaring that the perpetrator *wasn't one of us*—would ring out from households across the nation. That was a way of saying that the behavior being reported was out of character with the moral code established by the community, so it was highly unlikely that a member of the community had been involved. Back in the day, even street gangs adhered to a behavioral code that positioned harm to young children and the elderly as "off-limits." In contrast, look at the rampant and senseless violence that holds too many of our neighborhoods under siege today. There used to be a shared sense that there was a certain way to deal with one another.

Without strong character, it's impossible to establish the levels of trust needed to live in community with others. In authentic communities, each member is held accountable for rising to the standard of behaviors espoused in the moral code adopted by the community. And they are held responsible for their behavior when they do not. How else can the community thrive? There can be no growth without accountability. Character determines how people move through life, and it is an indicator of whether or not they can be counted on to honor personal bonds and act in the best interests of the community. It's the difference between those leaders who remain faithful to the interests of the community over time versus those who exploit their positions for personal gain, often at the expense of the community. We experience the fallout of these character gaps far too often. How many times have we been called upon to support elected officials who have pledged to serve their citizens, but who later become embroiled in scandal? (Pause right here and do your own "In Memoriam: Those We've Lost . . ." segment like they do at the Grammy Awards. It's too much!) Subjugating the interests of the community for personal or political gain has become commonplace. Why is it that no one seems to feel any sense of trepidation about violating our interests? It's not only politicians. What about the merchant bandits who sell poor quality foods in our communities while eating halal at home? Or the payday loan predators and insurance companies that repetitively rip off and redline Black and Brown communities? Or anyone else who exploits our pain for profit? Has our well-being become so inconsequential that no one feels accountable to do right by us? Once we reconnect to the power of living and operating in authentic community, we will do a better job of holding ourselves and others accountable.

COURAGE

Being in authentic community requires a significant degree of personal and moral courage. Establishing intimate bonds with others necessitates that we show up in the fullness of who we are. So, yes, we bring all of our innate wonder with us—but the rest of our complex and unfinished selfhood comes along too! It takes great personal courage to stand vulnerable among others and commit to cocreating safe spaces where we are both challenged and supported in our growth—spaces where compassionate truth-telling thrives, and the giving and receiving of honest feedback is seen as essential. Personal courage emboldens moral courage. You know who immediately comes to mind when I think about excellent examples of moral courage? The everyday women and men who participated in the 1955 Montgomery Bus Boycott. Sure, the leaders whose names we all know were courageous, too, but think about what it must have been like for regular folks who were willing to put it all on the line to bring a greater good to fruition.

Despite threats, violence, and other acts of open hostility, for 381 days this community walked in lockstep to protest bus segregation. They walked to school, work, and worship. They organized car pools. They raised money to purchase additional vehicles. They got up early and came home late, but they did not ride those buses! They rallied together to ensure that buses in the city of Montgomery rolled through the streets without them. They say that on many days, empty buses were seen passing through the streets. For this community of courageous women, men, and young people, dignity and human rights were worth the personal sacrifices required by their cause. Most of their names never made the headlines or history books. Yet today we fly on the wings of their sacrifice. These giants showed us how it's done. How do we restore moral courage in ourselves and one another?

COMMITMENT

The presence of an authentic community is also defined by the degree of commitment its members demonstrate to one another's well-being and to the viability of the community as a whole. Commitment allows authentic communities to persevere through good times and bad. It bonds the community together when affection wanes and disagreements mount. Commitment is the realization of the promise to be meaningfully present, even when doing so seems counterintuitive or inconvenient. It is devotion to the higher purpose being fulfilled through the life of the community.

Esme is a performance poet and dancer who is actively engaged in some creative collectives around the city where she lives. She recalled the tremendous frustration and disappointment that she felt when creative differences among a community of artists almost jeopardized an upcoming performance. "At one point," she said, "I could no longer contain myself and shouted out, 'Why are we here? Why did we come together to make this production happen in the first place?'" Esme's impassioned outburst caused a shift in the conversation.

You see, the idea of coming together to produce the One Love Peace II Concert (named after the 1978 event organized by Bob Marley and held at Kingston's National Stadium) had originated after another summer weekend of senseless gun violence had rocked the city, leaving the community further traumatized and more families in the throes of grief. Esme and her friends decided that they would come together and use their creative talents to take a stand. Through the concert, they aimed to honor the young lives that had been lost to violence and to foster healing among the survivors. "As we went around the room, remembering our original *why*, we were able to see just how silly we'd become," Esme explained. "Suddenly, our sanity was back. The focus was no longer on our personal preferences as artists. We reconnected with a purpose that was more meaningful than the diva and divo aspects of our personalities." Together they worked through their differences and fulfilled their commitment to deliver an extraordinary performance that was well received by the broader community.

REIGNITING THE SPIRIT OF COMMUNITY

Creating authentic communities provides sanctuary, mitigates harm, and assures us that we don't stand alone. Here no spectators are sitting on the sidelines, taking bets on whether or not we'll survive the storm. As the legendary Al Jarreau sang, "We're in This Love Together." Love isn't neutral about what happens to you. Love takes a position. In authentic community, there are no silent bystanders when things spiral out of control. Instead, there is a firm and collective commitment to breaking the fall. And when crash landings can't be averted, the authentic community is where our broken pieces are gathered and put back together again.

Our ancestors survived the Middle Passage, the physical and psychological torture of enslavement, Jim Crow, and a host of other inequities and indignities too numerous to name. Yet they were able to emerge with their humanity intact. They went on to build self-governing and self-sustaining communities. They were able to stand firm against injustice, bringing the segregated South to its knees and shifting global consciousness about U.S. race relations in the process. Our ancestors bravely journeyed during the Great Migration and, once again, raised families and built decent communities in new "up North" homelands—only to see those communities destroyed, yet again. Still, they dared to live, love, and build brighter futures for their progeny. They demonstrated extraordinary courage against protracted and intransigent odds, while remaining committed to our collective uplift. Therein lies the power of authentic community. Connection, character, courage, and commitment were more than mere abstractions to communities of yesteryear. These attributes were the concrete foundation upon which our foreparents lived their lives. How will we reignite the spirit of community today?

MEDITATIVE THOUGHT

I embrace the power of authentic community.

WISDOM PROTOCOL

On the micro level, contemplate a group of people with whom you are in authentic community. In what way are the attributes of authentic community demonstrated in your relationship with these individuals? Which, if any, qualities are lacking? What actions can you initiate to begin to foster growth? On the macro level, where do you see the attributes of authentic community being demonstrated most effectively? Where are these characteristics lacking? And what, if anything, must be done about their absence?

CHAPTER 21

I'm Not Your Hype Man

Sometimes people try to destroy you precisely because they recognize your power—not because they don't see it, but because they see it and they don't want it to exist.

—BELL HOOKS

The "hype man" is an iconic figure in hip-hop music. The term, in all of its male-gendered vaingloriousness, has entered mainstream cultural vernacular. The hype man comes out before the main attraction to stoke the crowd and ensure that the audience is pumped up and ready to rock the house as soon as the superstar sets foot onstage. A good hype man is like a cheer squad on steroids—warming up the audience and then fading into the background until needed again. The hype man is not an opening act. When watching the opening act, we understand that the artists or groups are on the pathway to their own stardom. We know there's a likelihood they'll be headlining the show one day. Not so with the hype man, who rarely becomes the star of the show—at least not *that* show. The very existence of the hype man is predicated on the ability to make the magic happen for someone else, making it nearly impossible for the person in that role to become established as a creative force in his or her own right. Consequently, when the hype man's creative energy begins to peak and refuses to continue being supplanted, he or she often has to move away and create new outlets where that creativity can flourish and take center stage. (Think Jay Z and Tupac.) That's when the real magic happens.

WHO ARE YOU?

Who are you: the "hype man" or the star of the show? Whether by nature or by nurture, women tend to be very supportive and caring toward others. We cherish our capacity to inspire and encourage those around us. These are positive attributes when expressed within healthy boundaries; but when our parameters are too loose, and we give away too much of ourselves, we risk getting lost in someone else's story. Left unchecked, we fall into the abyss of propping up the dreams of others at the expense of our own.

My friend Nima tells the story of how she once found herself suffocating in someone else's dream. When she was just beginning her career in broadcasting, she worked with a producer who was also a woman of color. The producer, a network veteran, would invite Nima to participate in projects as she was getting her feet wet at the network. Eagerly, Nima accepted the invitations and began to collaborate on projects. Nima brought her A-game to each assignment. She enthusiastically championed each project and regularly acknowledged the talents of her producer and the crew when discussing their projects with others. She believed in the importance of being a good team player. At first, things appeared to be just fine. Nima is a sharp, hard worker who, in very short order, began to excel in her role as a reporter.

One would think that witnessing Nima as she blossomed would have been a source of pride for the producer who had taken an early interest in her career. But that wasn't the case at all. As others began to notice Nima's talent, the producer became resentful. She would discourage Nima from taking on more significant assignments, the very thing that was required if her career was going to advance. Upon further exploration, and to her great dismay, she discovered that the producer—who had once positioned herself as an ally—had been actively working behind the scenes to short-circuit the opportunities extended to Nima because doing so would mean that Nima's talents would be leveraged on projects being lead by other producers. The producer saw in Nima a certain *je ne sais quoi* and had decided to hitch her three-wheeled wagon to Nima's rising star. She recognized Nima's power but feared its existence outside of her control, so she attempted to relegate Nima to a position of inferiority and treat her like a possession—a star only allowed to shine in the producer's galaxy.

Wise women understand the value of good mentorship. These relationships aren't always formally structured, and sometimes they emerge rather organically. It was with this understanding that Nima initially welcomed her relationship with the producer. However, because Nima knew what good mentorship looked like, she was able to discern the differences between quality mentorship and what her frenemy was serving up. Those of you who have been beneficiaries of strong mentorship know that there are times when a mentor may advise you to take a course of action or to decline certain opportunities. A good mentor will give you honest feedback on whether or not—from the mentor's perspective—you're ready to make a particular move. And sometimes what the mentor shares is not what you'd hoped to hear. Yet because of the earned trust and respect that you have for that individual, you weigh their counsel carefully before making a decision.

Mentors don't say one thing *to you* and another *about you* to others. They bring it all straight to you! A solid mentor enables your development and does not exploit your talents for personal gain. Ultimately, a real mentor respects your right to determine your own course. Above all else, a true mentor-mentee relationship is rooted in mutual respect, honesty, and transparency. What's the moral of the story? When you are blessed with a good mentoring relationship, honor it like the treasure it is! Also, realize that everyone who seeks to position herself as a mentor isn't automatically a quality mentor. Examine how the individual relates to you and not only what she says she's doing to support you. This is precisely what Nima did, and it was quite eye-opening.

MASTER THE LESSON

Here's a pattern that you'll recognize as a spiritual sojourner. The nature of the spiritual journey mandates that we always acknowledge and seek to understand the inner state that contributed to the outer condition. This is all about self-mastery. Yep, we've got to own our part in it! Have you ever wondered what's behind the self-sacrificing behaviors in which women often engage? For me, a significant root cause was the need for acceptance and approval. Sound familiar? I've been there, having once done time as the quintessential "go-to girl" for inspiration and motivation.

As a young woman, I was the friend who could be counted on to believe in the dream as much as the dreamer did. If you were down, I had uplifting words. If you were frightened, I'd mix up a bowl of courage. If you were feeling lost, I'd do my best to create the path and then light the way. My heart was earnest. My passion for life was absolutely infectious! I thought that by extending myself toward others I would be appreciated and respected. I hoped that if I supported the dreams of others, I'd be supported in kind. There were times when that was exactly what happened! In those instances, I cultivated wonderful friendships rooted in mutuality and respect. But it didn't always play out that way.

There were other times when I was met by those who sought to position me as appendages to their dreams, at the expense of fidelity to my own dreams. Inevitably, tensions would arise when I wouldn't capitulate. I was making the same mistake that many women do—giving too much of myself to those offering too little in return. I was misappropriating an essential spiritual principle: *Give what you want to receive.* What was missing at that time was the revelation of another spiritual principle: *You can't give what you don't have.* Because I was not operating from a base of inner power and self-acceptance, those attributes weren't reflected back to me. Consequently, since I hadn't yet taken possession of my own power with authority and dominion, I attracted into my experience people who sought to position me as appendages to their dreams. As I matured and became more confident in my own being, the need for external validation was relinquished. Barren and heavy-laden relationships began to fade away as new life-affirming relationships, more in harmony with the woman that I was becoming, took form. *As within, so without.* What spiritual truth underlies how your power is currently being expressed in your relationships?

HOLD UP

Have you had enough of subjugating your needs and desires to the needs and desires of others? Are you ready to own your power unapologetically? Are you up for the challenge of starring in your own life? Yes? Wonderful! Begin by assessing the quality of your primary relationships to determine whether or not you're the "hype man" of your crew. Pay attention to the quality of the exchanges you experience. The following questions will help you to focus: Is the love, honor, and respect that you extend returned to you? Are you giving value and receiving value from the relationship? Are your goals and dreams supported, or treated as peripheral? When you begin to make strides in some area of life, is your success celebrated or met with resentment?

Are you encouraged to rise high or to "stay in your place"? At the end of the day, is the relationship empowering or burdensome?

Answering the questions mentioned above will provide insight into the degree of mutuality present in your relationships. Simply stated, mutuality is the two-way flow of love, benefit, support, and sharing in a relationship. When these attributes are not present, mutuality cannot exist. In the absence of mutuality, conflict arises as a result of the tension caused by the imbalance in the relationship. Achieving mutuality in relationships requires that the involved parties possess a certain degree of integrity and wholeness. Only when you have cultivated adequate emotional and spiritual wellness are you able to support someone else in fully expressing their life's purpose without envy or fear that doing so somehow threatens your ability to do the same. Remember, those who are walking in authentic power will gladly support you in doing the same.

MEDITATIVE THOUGHT

I stand in my power and choose to star in my own life.

WISDOM PROTOCOL

1. Make a list of the areas in your life where you deny yourself full self-expression because of concerns about what others may think.
2. Make a list of how your approval-seeking behaviors show up in those situations.
3. Identify one thing you can do differently the next time you realize you're demonstrating that behavior.

CHAPTER 22

Speak Life

The best thing you can do is to be a woman
and stand before the world and speak your heart.

—ABBEY LINCOLN

Did you know that sound affects matter? The cells within our body actually respond to the vibrations of sound in the environment. This is why listening to different genres of music evokes different emotions. Listening to Lalah Hathaway feels different from listening to Buju Banton or Johann Sebastian Bach. Words and sounds are powerful. In sacred text, the creative power of words is credited with calling existence into being—a spiritual metaphor guiding us to recognize and harness the "Let there be . . ." creative power that resides within each of us.

Are the words you speak in harmony with the life you seek to live? Your words are a powerful creative force. They spring forth from your heart, take root in your consciousness, and ultimately bear fruit in your world. When we embrace that we are literally "speaking into being" the situations and circumstances of our lives, we become more mindful of what comes out of our mouths. The delicious, soulful power of a woman's words can affirm life, invoke healing, and create peace. But that same tongue, unbridled and on fire, can deny peace, negate joy, and foster discord. A wise woman strives to remain in integrity with her words—those she speaks over her own life and into the lives of others.

When we are in integrity with our words, we *consciously* own what we say by committing to a degree of thoughtfulness before we part our lips. We remember that it's not only the words but also the heartspace from which they are spoken that matters. For most of us, our relationship with words is unsteady. We speak with confidence and authority over those areas of our lives where power and possibilities are already evident. And that's not a bad thing. In fact, affirming your already-present good is a wonderful practice. But what about those areas where we have experienced greater challenge and the good isn't easily seen? What do you say to yourself about the beloved dream you once held close that today seems to be perpetually deferred? In these instances, our words often falter. But it's precisely in those very desolate places that we must bring the creative power of our words to bear.

When Nola and Paul came together to form a family, it was not without complexities. He came with two teen daughters who were still in the process of healing after their parents' contentious divorce. Two younger children, a niece and nephew, accompanied Nola. She had become their mom after their birth mother's battle with drug addiction rendered her unable to care for them. Two years earlier, a stray bullet had taken their father—Nola's older brother—away from them and torn their lives apart. Between the six of them, the emotional stew was thick. Still, Nola envisioned something beautiful coming into being, a deep longing to love and be loved, and she was determined to bring it to fruition. Unable to physically bear children of her own, Nola fully embraced motherhood as a sacred soul assignment. This was her divine path, and she approached it as such.

It was at the wedding reception that Nola received her first taste of just how rocky the road would be. Paul's two daughters approached her after she'd touched a nerve by introducing them to a guest as her daughters. The eldest spoke first and firmly: "Just because you married our father doesn't make you our mother. We already have a mother, Miss Nola." The second daughter added, "And we don't want to babysit your kids, so please don't ask." They then turned around in unison and sashayed away. She maintained her cool, but it took Nola a minute to forgive herself for what she *really* wanted to say in that moment. In fact, it was then that their nicknames, Thing 1 and Thing 2, were born. Nola never spoke those nicknames aloud, but she held them close to heart for whenever levity was needed.

The first couple of years were stormy. Miscommunication abounded, tempers flared, and patience wore paper-thin as her blended family struggled to push past the pain and doubt to find a way forward together. All the while, Nola spoke life over her family: "My family is healthy, happy, and whole. Jah bless." She understood the importance of holding firmly to the vision of a loving family, even when appearances suggested otherwise. This was reflected in her prayers and in her interactions with her loved ones. Nola's words were the blueprints from which her family began to build. By keeping the energy and vibrations of her words lifted she was—in fact—raising the frequency of her current situation to match that of the reality that she wanted to experience. Nola understood that the words that she spoke in the present moment would someday greet her in the future.

Together, she and her husband worked to create a harmonious home environment that would serve as an incubator for the life that they were building. Understanding the relationship between good nutrition and overall physical and emotional well-being, the family adhered to strict Ital dietary standards—forgoing processed foods, additives, sugar, and iodized table salt while consuming as many natural foods as possible. Nola and Paul established "contributions," a series of daily tasks that were assigned to each member of the household. Even the younger children were responsible for age-appropriate contributions, such as helping to pack the next day's lunches. They didn't want their children to grow up thinking that an orderly home just happens. It was vital for them to understand that each member must contribute to creating a home life in which the family can thrive. Nola and Paul provided the love, discipline and consistency required for their burgeoning family to flourish.

These outer actions were reflections of the inner dialogue (word) and mental attitude (mind) embodied by Nola and Paul. In other words, their daily life was the outworking of their mental and emotional energies on the physical plane. Over time, their life together began to reflect more and more of the attributes that had been envisioned and called forth. Fear and discord gave way to trust and harmony. The older girls opened their hearts to Nola and created a welcoming space for her there. They embraced their younger siblings and became very protective of them. Emotional and spiritual healing was evident on all fronts. Word became flesh and a "healthy, happy and whole" family was created. This beautiful family is still going strong today.

Through Nola's example, we are reminded of the power of words. Wise women use this power to speak life, heal brokenness, and call all manner of good into being. A wise woman employs her faculty of imagination to see beyond the temporal experiences in front of her and envisions life through the lens of a higher truth. She understands that the words that she speaks are emanations of what she holds in her heart and mind—creations that will at some point return to her as fulfilled desire. Accordingly, she chooses her words carefully and wields her creative power thoughtfully. Sisters, I bear witness that if you embrace and apply the principles outlined in this essay—your life will be transformed in the most magnificent ways. But, don't take my word for it. Put them into practice and see for yourself. I bid you Godspeed. May your words prosper and bear good fruit.

MEDITATIVE THOUGHT

Every word I speak, and every thought I think, shapes my reality. I speak life.

WISDOM PROTOCOL

What are you creating with your words? Assess the degree to which you consistently remain in integrity with your words. Does your inner conversation reflect the highest vision for your life? Next, think about how your words impact those around you. Do others feel strengthened and supported by your words? If not, what will you do to wield the creative power of your words more constructively?

CHAPTER 23

That Kind of Beauty

The kind of beauty I want most is the hard-to-get kind that comes from within—strength, courage, dignity.

—RUBY DEE

Have you ever been deeply moved by the power of an image? As a collector of art and photography, I am keenly aware of the feelings invoked by certain images. It's true: A great picture really is worth a thousand words. One of my all-time favorite photographs was captured in 1963 by Gordon Parks, one of my favorite photographers. It's entitled *Ethel Sharrieff* and named after the woman who elegantly stands front and center. Ethel Sharrieff served as the national captain of the Muslim Girls Training and General Civilization Classes (MGT and GCC), a specialized curriculum taught to girls and women in the Nation of Islam that is designed to impart wisdom, knowledge, and cultural refinement. The image was originally published as part of a photographic essay, "*What Their Cry Means to Me*"—*A Negro's Own Evaluation*, which Parks created for *Life* magazine. In the iconic black-and-white photograph, Ethel Sharrieff and her charges are standing in a V-formation. The juxtaposition of row after row of graceful Black female bodies adorned in white from head to toe is quite poignant. What stands out, even more than the striking composition of the photograph, is the dignity and strength that the image exudes. The "all clear" gaze emanating from the face of Sister Instructress, as Ethel Sharrieff was lovingly called, is moving. Precisely the kind of beauty that Mama Ruby speaks of in the epigraph of this chapter. How do we cultivate that type of hard-to-get beauty within ourselves? Restoration is the key.

Have you ever marveled at the beauty of a mosaic glass vase? This elegant artistic creation is achieved by gluing pieces of shattered glass onto a solid base. The asymmetry of the individual pieces comes together to make an interesting and aesthetically pleasing work of art. The shattered glass, having been appropriately repurposed, finds new and radiant life. Thus, the mosaic glass vase is an apt metaphor for the way in which the broken pieces of our lives, when affixed to our spiritual foundation, craft us into more intricate and beautiful beings. Without a secure foundation, however, we're left with lots of scattered, sharp edges that pose a danger to us and all who cross our path.

Finding the right foundation is crucial, though we sometimes take a somewhat circuitous route to discovering it. Some seek to find wholeness in the outer world of people and things. They reason that with the right credentials, the right vehicle, or the perfect trophy spouse, they can hide the scars beneath their polished public personas. They strive and they climb and they acquire, only to reach the pinnacle and discover that all of the Prada on Oak Street can't eradicate the mountain of self-doubt and insecurities that remain unhealed. The bandage may look pretty, but it simply won't hold. The only way to confront brokenness is to commit to healing. The transmutation of gaping and painful wounds into testimonial scars only happens when we accept responsibility for healing and pursue wholeness in partnership with the Creator.

Emotional healing is deeply personal work that can't be accomplished by proxy. A good therapist can be an excellent facilitator of healing, but she can't do the work for you. Your lover can't kiss it away, and your friends can't throw it away on your behalf. The loving-kindness of others can be a soothing balm that helps to clear away the debris that covers the wounds, thereby making it easier for you to explore what's there. But no one, no matter how much they wish they could, can do for you what only you can do for yourself.

Here's the dilemma: The sensitive nature of some wounds causes us to resist committing to their healing. This hesitation is not without cause. The pursuit of healing can be complicated, time-consuming, and draining. The only thing more arduous is continuing to live with wounds that sit silently gaping and unaddressed. Inner wounds don't go away because we suppress them. They merely lie dormant until some experience taps into their tenderness and reminds us of their need for care. There is no easy out. Our wounds must be healed by our own hands.

For much of her adult life, Violet refused to explore the impact that the sexual abuse she experienced during her youth was having on her adult relationships. She fervently believed that by not discussing what had happened she could effectively deny those experiences the power to hold any sway over her life. But, of course, the opposite occurred. The aftermath of the abuse not only touched her relationships but also created barriers to the intimacy she desired. Violet's first marriage, years earlier, had ended in divorce. Many culprits—some of her creation and others of his—were responsible for the demise of the marriage. After remaining single for a number of years without involvement in a long-term, committed relationship, Violet met Curtis, and it nearly scared her to death.

This man was everything she'd prayed for in a life partner. He was kind, smart, and ambitious. Even more importantly, he was a genuinely caring soul who was fully present and emotionally available to her. He came offering partnership and the mature type of love she'd been seeking. She wasn't concerned about not being able to connect with him sexually. She'd long since developed a sexual persona that allowed her to distance her physical self from her emotional self. But there were many layers to her interior life that she'd kept hidden from view. Violet feared not being able to bring her most authentic self to the relationship she wanted to experience fully, and that led her to seek counseling.

After months of working with her therapist, Violet decided to tell Curtis about the abuse in her past. She worried that he might see her differently and actually look down upon her. She worried that he might find her less desirable once her secret was exposed. The shame sat high in her chest as she began to share her story with him. Bravely, she poured out the details of the abuse she had endured and its aftermath, which had pained her for years. Curtis proved himself to be every bit of the man she'd held him up to be. Violet described his response as the most generous and sincere act of compassion she'd ever experienced.

Those moments, when she first stood emotionally naked in front of her beloved, proved to be pivotal in shaping the deep intimacy that they would go on to share as a couple. Later, Violet reflected that it was only after opening herself up to Curtis and trusting him with her truth that she was able to put her protective sexual persona to rest. Once she was able to show up authentically and vulnerably, she experienced lovemaking with her husband in ways that were succulent and new.

Violet carried anguish that was rooted in sexual abuse. And though that's not a burden we all have to carry, we can most certainly find aspects of her journey that mirror our own. Every woman has some part of herself that demands the application of great strength, courage, and compassion in order to be restored. Here are some important points to remember as we pursue revitalization in whatever area requires care. There is a part of us that is entirely free of the hurt of any experience we've ever had. It is absolutely whole and complete, wide-awake, and aware. Untouched and untattered by the experiences of the human journey. It's our natural essence—the very core of who we are. That's our base and our most enduring aspect. It is the sturdy foundation that undergirds all healing.

Sometimes achieving the breakthrough we seek requires that we enlist the support of others. When this is the case, we must, like Violet, take the leap and seek solace in the listening ear of a caring friend, family member, or professional healer. Too often we allow shame to hold us hostage. We fear being judged or ridiculed, so we try to go it alone. That's not wisdom! Don't let false pride and unhealthy attachments to what others may think keep you from reaching out for the support you need. Investing in your emotional well-being not only aids in the healing of past hurts, but also it lessens your vulnerability to future injury. Commit today to living the joy-filled life you deserve. Pursuing greater wholeness is an integral part of your life purpose. You are worth every bit of energy that it takes to heal your wounds. Anything less than loving yourself enough to invest in your own healing is dancing on shattered glass.

MEDITATIVE THOUGHT

My greatest beauty comes from within.
I am committed to my own healing.

WISDOM PROTOCOL

1. Identify an emotional wound that needs healing in your life.
2. Determine what type of support you'd like to receive

on your healing journey. Do you want to share your experience with a loved one, friend, support group, or counseling professional? What outcome do you hope to receive?

3. Commit to taking the first step toward your healing by reaching out to the person or group you identified above within the next seventy-two hours.

CHAPTER 24

Dream a New Dream

You are never too old to set another goal
or to dream a new dream.

—C.S. LEWIS

Sometimes we get caught dreaming dreams that were never designed to bring us peaceful rest. In fact, these dreams weren't designed for us at all. When this happens, it's imperative that we muster the courage to dream a new dream. Several years ago, I was invited to dinner at the home of my colleague Devi and her husband, Anil. Their home, like the others in the Bloomfield Hills subdivision, boasted beautiful architectural design and a picture-perfect lawn. The community is in an affluent suburb of Detroit, rife with stunning homes and noted for its quality schools. Anil and Devi lived on the lower level of the home with their two children and Devi's mother, who resided with them for half the year and in New York for the remainder. During the evening, as the conversation progressed, the couple talked about their unique living arrangement.

It turned out that three families occupied the home at that time. The lower unit, home to Devi and Anil's family, was laid out like a moderately sized ranch home. There was a great room, comprised of a living and dining area, a modern chef's kitchen, a game room, three bedrooms, two full bathrooms, and an expansive outdoor veranda. The upper levels of the home were occupied by two other families who shared the common areas. Each family was responsible for paying one-third of the monthly lease amount. The home had been purchased by an East Indian community service organization for the distinct purpose of facilitating economic independence among community members. Families applied to live in the home by presenting a financial goal, and a realistic plan for achieving it, before a review committee. If approved for residency, the family moved into the home and shared expenses with the other families until the goal was met, within the agreed upon timeframe. Then they would move out so the next family could move in and reap the benefits of the communal housing arrangement.

Devi and Anil were saving funds to purchase a home. The savings they would accrue over the three years of their stay in the communal property would allow them to place a hefty down payment on a modest home of their own in the same area. They anticipated that they would be able to pay off the new home mortgage within five years, instead of the typical fifteen to thirty years. Together, the couple had envisioned a life for themselves that was free from the constraints of conspicuous consumption. They dreamed a dream of being mortgage-free and financially at ease. They were willing to take the steps necessary to bring their long-range goals into fruition.

What about you? What is your dream for your financial future? Have you examined your current financial practices to determine whether they are leading you down the path of sweet dreams or toward night terrors? Do your daily practices align with your dream? If not, what changes are necessary?

Bedazzled dreams are marketed to us every day, but it's up to us to determine whether or not to take the bait. The problem with squatting in someone else's dream is that the dream may or may not be beneficial to you. Unless your circumstances closely mirror the dreamer's, chances are you won't experience the same results trying to follow the dreamer's path. Think about the big house and the Birkin bag. Is that really your dream, or is that the dream of the marketing team that designed the ad aimed at selling you a certain picture of success? And if that really is your dream, how will you pursue it in a manner that positions you for prosperity and long-term success?

Don't be afraid to dream a new dream. Allow yourself to reconnect with the wisdom of our foremothers who were bigger savers than consumers. Remember Mother Oseola McCarty, the eighty-seven-year-old washerwoman from Hattiesburg, Mississippi, who saved over $150,000 and donated it to the University of Southern Mississippi to provide scholarships for Black students. She desired to provide for others the opportunity for education that she never had. She was a woman who chose the fulfillment of purpose over the accumulation of possessions. She lived frugally and saved for decades in order to make her gift a reality. Her legacy will live on through the lives she has transformed with her gift.

Channel the wisdom of our mothers who always had some type of entrepreneurial venture going on the side. Whether it was styling hair, hemming skirts, or managing the accounting books at the local dry cleaners, they knew how to keep those extra coins coming. Long before the term *passive income* was popular, these savvy women were putting the principle of having multiple income streams to work. There is much to learn from the strength of their example.

Dare to dream a new dream, and boldly commit yourself to making it a reality.

MEDITATIVE THOUGHT

I am the dreamer of new dreams!

WISDOM PROTOCOL

Identify three specific and measurable financial goals that you would like to achieve over the next year. Write down the steps you will take. Identify an accountability partner who will support you as you work toward your goals.

SUITE THREE

Reawakening

Woke

Dear God,
With my whole heart,
I seek you.
With my whole self,
I surrender to the
joy,
peace,
wisdom,
faith, hope, and love
reawakening inside of me.
Let it be.

CHAPTER 25

The Awakened Consciousness

To love. To be loved. To never forget your own insignificance. To never get used to the unspeakable violence and the vulgar disparity of life around you. To seek joy in the saddest places. To pursue beauty to its lair. To never simplify what is complicated or complicate what is simple. To respect strength, never power. Above all, to watch. To try and understand. To never look away. And never, never to forget.

—ARUNDHATI ROY

THE NATURE OF AWAKENING

I used to experience a recurring dream in which I would find myself standing in the main room of a beautiful home, looking at all of the aesthetically pleasing features and furnishings of the room. Being in that space felt warm and wonderful. The colors, textures, and even the smell of the room were spectacular. It was the most exquisite room I'd ever seen. As my eyes wandered from the intricately crafted crown molding to an amazing abstract painting, I noticed a door. Brimming with curiosity, I excitedly made my way to the door to peek inside. Slowly, I turned the knob and gazed into the next room. I was completely blown away! This room was even more amazing than the first. How could this be? It was as if the first room was merely a preview of something far grander. The second room was more spacious, more nuanced, and more elegant in every way. My heartbeat quickened as I took it all in. And then I saw yet another door. As the dream progressed, I continued through a series of entries, each about the size of a standard bedroom door, only to discover increasingly beautiful and more expansive spaces behind each one. It never ended—the wonder went on and on.

THE BIG AHA!

This dream occurred during a time in my life when I was acutely focused on discovering the divine purpose for my life. *What am I here to do?* was the question I carried on my heart and into my prayers. Through this dream, the Holy Spirit revealed the answer. I am here to experience greater and greater revelations of the Divine's presence, and power as the Universal Life Force lives through me. The rooms in the dream represented the expansion of consciousness that occurs on the journey to greater enlightenment. It all clicked! A sense of clarity washed over me. As the relationship with Spirit deepens and consciousness expands, we move from glory to glory in every way. Through this process of ascended consciousness, we are able to give birth to our dreams and allow them to take flight. The pathway to purposeful living isn't solely about what we're here to do, but also who we're here to become.

Without question, there is a divine plan for each and every one of our lives. The creative force that purposed a sun to light the day sky and a moon to rule the night is the same force that created you. The Infinite Intelligence that designed, with great intricacy, the human body, is the same intelligence that designed you. Just as each of the organs, systems, cells, and elements of the body has a distinct purpose, so do you. Examples abound in nature and within the animal kingdom of the tremendous care taken to ensure that all of creation was positioned to serve and sustain this experience that we call life. As Spirit reveals itself through each of us, we become open vessels that can be used in service to the unfoldment of a greater good—and the opportunities to do so appear. In the words of scripture, God has "*plans* to prosper *you* and not to harm *you*, *plans* to give *you* hope and a future." But it's up to us to cultivate the consciousness needed to experience and express the full bounty of those plans. It is from that sacred ground that we can begin to ask: *What gifts am I here to give? What impact am I here to have on my family, my community, and the world?*

Once you're awake, you know. And once you know, you become responsible. One of the hallmarks of an awakened consciousness is the realization that individual consciousness is a contributor to collective consciousness. The principle of oneness doesn't just extend itself to our connectedness to the sunrise, ocean waves, and other wonders of creation. The other stuff is us too—a fact often ignored during the earlier stages of our spiritual development as we focus on shifting our mindsets to create changes in our personal lives.

We become much more powerful vessels for change in the outer world as our inner world is healed. Often, and rightfully so, we direct our attention to the gross patterns of disharmony evident in the broader society. Yet until we recognize and eradicate the insidious, unconscious attachment to disharmony in our personal lives, our capacity to effectively establish harmony, balance, and order in our shared world is compromised. The collective consciousness of a society creates the out-picturing of the prevailing mindsets of the individuals who make up that society. When we no longer have a tolerance for gross imbalance and disharmony in our heads, hearts, and homes, we will create a society in which the horrors of Chicago's

"Wild Hundreds," and the Charleston Massacre cannot exist. Our shift in the collective consciousness will create a tipping point from which we will demand and build something better for ourselves, our children, and those who will inherit the world we leave behind.

I'M NEW HERE

Have you ever noticed the distinct quality of voice that women acquire when they awaken to their power? It's a sound vibration borne of prescient clarity of thought, calmness of spirit, and certainty of self and purpose. Perhaps you've noticed the vocal quality I'm describing in women you have observed. Maybe you're beginning to notice it more and more in yourself. From within the purview of the awakening consciousness the way that you see the world shifts. Some days you may even ask yourself, *Why didn't I notice that before?* Irrevocably healed from the pattern of unseeing or selective sight, your awareness of life will blossom in ways never before experienced. Your senses, no longer obstructed by the mindless obsessions of the mental world that you used to inhabit, are magnified. You'll hear the subtext in conversations even when the words remain unspoken. You'll obtain insight into people and situations by merely stilling yourself and feeling into them. The everyday beauty of the sunrise will move you to tears, and the day-to-day ugliness of the unhealed world will call you to action.

You're not the same woman you used to be. The distinction between personal restoration and an awakened state of consciousness is the capacity to translate the deep knowing borne of individual transformation into an act of sacred service. That wonderful bounty of spiritual growth you have cultivated can now be leveraged to benefit the world in some meaningful way. The wise woman who has reawakened to her higher nature carries the same question on her heart each day: *How will I allow Spirit to express through me today?* We exist to reveal the Divine through the expression of our distinctive gifts and talents.

The Reflective Essays, Meditative Thoughts, and Wisdom Protocols in this section focus on the attributes of the awakened consciousness and invite you to stretch yourself by putting your unique talents and gifts to work in the outer world. When you consciously live from a place of faith, balance, generosity, truth, order, harmony, and justice, you see the world differently. You take notice of things that previously may have only existed on the periphery of your consciousness. Which issues matter the most to you? What would you like to see different in the world? The exercises in this section of the book are designed to facilitate contemplation and action and to support you in becoming clearer about the ways in which your unique attributes and experiences can be used in the fulfillment of your purpose. Pay attention to how you respond to each exercise. Which feel natural and free-flowing? Which are more challenging for you? What support do you need to move from your current level of expression to the next?

The road to your awakened life may feel a bit uneven at times. At least, that's how it was for me. This is to be expected. You've changed, but many of the people and situations that are a part of your world of affairs may not have changed to the same degree or moved in the same direction. There may be times when you find yourself caught up in the vibrational pull of ways of thinking or being that are remnants of your former self. If that should happen, just remind yourself of why you're committed to the unfoldment of the wise woman within. One of the observations that I made during the early stages of my own journey was that there were certain environments I could only take in small doses. Just as it wouldn't be wise to spend an hour in a smoke-filled room and expect not to smell like smoke when you walked out, it's unwise to believe you can spend substantial amounts of time in environments that are not aligned with the life you're creating and not be adversely affected. Whenever you miss the mark, simply take aim again. As you stay the course on your transformational journey, your spiritual stamina will increase, and you will be better able to ward off regressive distractions. Also, remember to revisit the earlier sections of the book. Don't hesitate to go back to the Reflective Essays, Meditative Thoughts, and Wisdom Protocols that have proven to be especially useful when you find yourself falling back into pesky mental or behavioral habits.

CHAPTER 26

Pagan Poetry

Until the killing of black men, black mothers' sons, becomes as important to the rest of the country as the killing of a white mother's son—we who believe in freedom cannot rest.

—ELLA BAKER

When did you stop counting? Was it the news about Rekia Boyd or Tamir Rice? Or was it when you heard about Sandra Bland? Or Michael Brown? Philando Castile? Keith Lamont Scott, or Stephon Clark? At what point did it start feeling like too much? Was it when you realized that the plights of Cecil, the lion and Harambe, the silverback gorilla had inspired a greater outcry than the sixteen shots that blazed through the body of Laquan McDonald? Was that it? Or was it when nine-year-old Tyshawn Lee was lured away from a neighborhood playground to his execution? Maybe it was when you remembered that Relisha Rudd is still missing and wondered why so few seem to care when sweet, little Black girls and Black women vanish into thin air. When were you first aware of the can't stop, won't stop rhythm of your tears? *Tōēbā* is the Hebrew word from which the English translation *abomination* is derived. The term is used to denote a severe moral offense. If you're like me, you're probably struck by how commonplace these offenses have become. Barely a day goes by when we don't witness such egregious acts. In fact, they've become so ordinary that often we're no longer awakened by their overbearing presence. But awaken we must!

Take a look around you and see just how quickly you can check them off. The hubris of an oil company CEO who just wants to "get on with his life" after the oil spill that happened on his watch left people and the ecosystem struggling for survival. The politician whose twisted tongue has landed her in court on corruption charges. War, war, and more war decimating the lives of innocent children, women, and men in every corner of the globe. Dead children, fallen like soldiers, in the hearts of our cities. Scheming executives who plotted to gain exorbitant profits, who knew that their actions would have devastating long-term consequences for the rest of us, effectively wiping out the generational wealth of entire communities. The friend who's quick to call to share about someone else's hardship, eager to report what she perceives as "bad news." People everywhere who know the truth about something, yet do not reveal it—opting instead to procure some manner of personal reward in exchange for their silence. Folks who always "wanna be starting something," who create grief for someone else in a misguided attempt to get relief from the misery of their own lives.

Pagan poetry. The beautifully styled yet meaningless mutterings of a world that lives in service to a lesser god. Proclamations of righteousness, justice, peace, and love ring out often and loudly, while new altars are continually being erected to the gods of indifference, dehumanization, war, greed, intolerance, and other abominations too plentiful and too painful to name. Sometimes the darkness is so profound that the light seems irreversibly obscured.

LIGHT IT UP!

Is it numbness or indifference? Denial or deep despair? What does one make of the cavalier manner people have toward incidents that demonstrate the systemic devaluation of Black life? How should we interpret the "as the beat goes on" mentality that appears to be unmoved by the harsh winds of injustice? Has the very core of humanity blown away as well, or was it buried long ago? Is the chasm between us so great that empathy and compassion have fallen in the bowels of our shared and complicated history? These are the questions that I find myself asking each time a Black body is needlessly sacrificed—and aside from those who also inhabit Black bodies, few seem to care.

It might be tempting to turn away. To distance oneself from the rush of emotions—hurt, fear, and raging anger—that pulse through our veins. No matter what others may or may not do, we must not flee. We must not walk around as if nothing is terribly wrong. Why are flags not flying at half-staff across this land? Is it because Ella's words still ring true? The killing of Black men and women, Black mothers' sons and daughters, is not yet as important as the killing of white men and white mothers' sons. Don't allow yourself to go numb. It's the ostrich-in-the-sand coping mechanism that got us here. The long-standing history of racism and violence against Black people and other people of color will not magically go away if we just pretend it doesn't exist. Moral blight cannot be cleansed by our refusal to see it. These complicated and complex ethical, social, and political issues deserve our rapt attention and purposeful action.

Wise women don't turn away from the uncomfortable and uneven places that leave us searching for steady ground. We do not give in to despair. Or hatred. Or indifference. Wise women go within to access the wisdom and courage needed to transform the conditions around us. Our inner work equips us to create meaningful change in the outer world. We are humble enough to learn from history and the soundness of our elders. We are spiritually attuned enough to channel the energies of the great mothers who have gone before us. We rise on the wings of:

Dr. Maya's wisdom,
Zora's realness,
and the fierceness of Fannie Lou.
We invoke Sojourner's Truth,
Shirley's strength,
Rosa's determination,
and the courage of Ida B.
We dance in Ella's brilliance,
and above *all* else,
We give light,
and people find the way.

The world needs your light and mine! There's work for each of us to do. One woman may find herself at the forefront of a major mobilization effort to implement community policing programs, while another woman takes it upon herself to regularly create senior safety circles in her community. One woman organizes a meditation class for youth, while you start a community garden. No expression of sacred activism is too big or too small. It's all necessary and vital. Be faithful to the gifts inside of you and bring them to the fore. Identify an area where your contribution is needed and then put your unique gifts and talents to work.

MEDITATIVE THOUGHT

I am the light that illumines
the pathway to a new world.

WISDOM PROTOCOL

Make a list of your gifts and talents. Consider the places around you where your contributions could make a difference. Identify one action you will take to give light to a space where darkness currently reigns.

CHAPTER 27

Paint the Picture, Write the Book, Do the Thing

But you can't have people say, "I'm going to wait to get into Carnegie Hall. Neighborhoods should have institutions to support their own."

—MARJORIE ELIOT

The building itself is wondrous. Proudly commanding the corner of 160th Street and Edgecombe Avenue in Manhattan, the 555 is an architectural and cultural gem. Boasting a striking Beaux-Arts architecture, complete with a Tiffany glass-domed and marble lobby, the 555—or the Triple Nickel, as it is popularly known—has served as a vortex of African-American creative and intellectual genius for much of her hundred-year existence. Beginning in the 1940s, successful Blacks began to set up residence in the Washington Heights neighborhood, which sits north of Sugar Hill. Some community members prefer to describe the area as the northern tip of Harlem. Since that time a number of notable figures have called the 555 home including:

- Eslanda Goode Robeson (noted Pan-Africanist scholar, anthropologist, activist, and author) and her husband, Paul Robeson (actor, attorney, singer, and activist)
- Rose Morgan (beauty entrepreneur) and her husband, Joe Louis (legendary boxer)
- Drs. Mamie Phipps Clark and Kenneth Clark and (scholars and social psychologists best known for their "doll studies," which provided empirical evidence of the deleterious effects of white supremacy on the self-esteem of Black children)
- Count Basie (jazz musician and composer)
- Canada Lee (actor and composer)

Are you feeling the Triple Nickel vibe? The rich heritage of this community continues to thrive today through the lives of artists and innovators, such as the incomparable Ms. Marjorie Eliot.

Every Sunday afternoon for over twenty years, Marjorie Eliot has hosted parlor jazz concerts in her home at the 555. Jazz aficionados from down the way, across the Hudson, and around the globe eagerly and tightly fill her spacious apartment. A profusion of carefully placed folding chairs transform the living quarters into an intimate concert hall. Piano. Bass. Brass. Magic. At 3:30 p.m., the musicians begin to play. As the rich tones and intricate rhythms fill the air, parlor guests bear witness to the power of the experience. Eyes closed, heads swaying. Feet tapping. Bodies rocking, hands waving. Rapt stillness. This continues for two hours, with intermittent breaks for bursts of applause. The afternoon ends with the performance of original theatrical readings authored by Ms. Eliot. From beginning to end, the entire experience is exquisite.

An emissary of what she defines as African-American classical music, Marjorie Eliot grew up in a home and community where music was central to living—a constant and healing presence in daily life. Indeed, the parlor concerts have been integral to her own healing. A striking woman of rich sepia tones and chiseled features, this talented musician is also a mother who has buried three of her five children. The weekly concerts afford her an opportunity to celebrate their lives and speak their names: Philip, Michael, and Alfie. When her fingers dance across the piano keyboard, the passion with which she plays reverberates throughout the apartment, filling it with what can only be described as sonic love. Marjorie Eliot is the real deal. In addition to producing the weekly concert series, she also teaches music classes and is an accomplished stage actress who once toured in a production of *No Place to Be Somebody*, the Pulitzer Prize-winning play by the renowned race-conscious dramatist Charles Gordone. A stunning example of purposeful living, Marjorie Eliot is a real inspiration.

What are you waiting for? Is it the right work, the right money, or the right connection? Ms. Marjorie didn't wait for Carnegie Hall to call; she established a high-quality concert hall right there in her living room. Now some of the same patrons who travel to Midtown for performances make the trek uptown to her place. She built, and they came. And they've been coming ever since!

Do you sometimes find yourself thinking that life will be just fine once you start your own business, get the children out of the house, and Prince Idris drops to one knee? Sometimes we impose unnecessary conditions on when, where, and how our life's purpose will unfold. Sometimes we wait endlessly for some validation outside of our own knowing. But the wise woman sojourner knows better. She centers herself and goes within. There she communes with Spirit and seeks guidance on the best way to make use of her gifts and talents. She listens for insights and revelations. Signs and subtle wonders. Then she moves into action! The path may not be perfectly clear. Her actions may not make sense to anyone else at the moment, but that's okay. She continues building the ark anyway. Fueled by a loving heart and an earnest desire to fulfill her life's purpose, she steps out in faith and trusts that the road ahead will lead to the life seeking expression through her.

So paint the picture, write the book, do the thing that you love to do. And whatever you do, dedicate it to the ever-present force for good and watch as the heavens conspire to bring forth your good.

MEDITATIVE THOUGHT

The time is now. I move in the direction of my purpose with ease and grace.

WISDOM PROTOCOL

Spend time in your sacred space thinking about one action you can take to begin moving in the direction of your purpose. If a clearly defined purpose hasn't yet been revealed to you, think about a skill, talent, or gift that you possess that can be used in service to others and start there.

CHAPTER 28

God's Got You

There is always the polarity: the right side, the left side; the day side, the night side. We on one side see suffering and pain, but on the other side we see giving, we see kindness, we see sympathy. We see a humanity opening its heart, its spirit, and reaching out to those who are in pain . . . mankind has to experience the truth of its humanity.

—ALICE COLTRANE

Sometimes it seems as if the sirens of disaster are screaming all around us. Calamity and chaos show up unexpectedly and shake the foundation of our faith: The sudden onset of a grave illness or the unanticipated ending of a relationship you thought would last forever. The loss of a job or a home. Hurricanes, tsunamis, earthquakes, and oil spills come to us, uninvited and unwelcomed, jarring us loose from stability. Casting us squarely on the shores of strange and forbidden lands. *How did I get here?* you ask as the shock slowly begins to dissipate. *What do I do now?* you contemplate as you initiate your search for meaning and direction.

Loving and seeking God doesn't exempt us from trial and tribulation. They are part of the human journey. We will experience pain, though we need not suffer. Tears will inevitably fall, but we need not drown in them. Our hearts will grieve loss, but we need not despair. Life will bring what it brings, but we will *not* be overtaken, for our confidence and sanctuary lie in power far greater than the human self.

Odelia is one of those people whose smile can be seen from a mile away! She and her family have been through some things that would have left others bitter and disheartened, but not Odelia and her crew. After losing the home to Hurricane Katrina that had housed her family for three generations, she and her family relocated to Houston. Just as the trauma of displacement and having to rebuild began to subside, one of her children was diagnosed with a debilitating anxiety disorder that meant she would need a specialized school. Finding the right school was neither quick nor easy, but Odelia persisted until she found a program that could meet her child's needs. When her husband was laid off, finances were tight for a while. But the family pulled back on spending and pressed through until things were better. She acknowledges that things have been tough, but she's never surrendered to despair.

When asked how she maintains her infectious optimism, she explains: "God has proven himself to me too many times for me to give up on him now. He's got me, and that's all I need to know to keep moving ahead!" She spoke of the generosity she witnessed after the storm, of the kind volunteers who traveled from across the globe to be part of relief efforts. The generosity of the sorority that collected and distributed gently used clothing, and the loving care demonstrated by the medical relief teams who were on-site during the early days of the disaster. Odelia recounted how her mounting apprehensions about moving to a city where they knew no one were eased when she first met Janine and James, heads of the family that hosted her family upon their arrival in Houston. "They were warm and made us feel welcome," she said. "That's not always the case when people know that you're coming with nothing. They were instrumental in helping us to get established in Houston. We're friends now. Always will be." Odelia continued,

> *A storm that takes away everything except your life isn't the kind of thing you plan for. For a long time, we were in shock as we went through the motions of trying to put our lives back together. But, every step of the way, there were hands outstretched to help us. People who didn't know us, or anything about us, made our well-being their business. And I know that was nothing but grace.*

Trying to navigate the rugged terrain of life on one's own accord is like marching swiftly onto a bed of quicksand. Drowning is imminent. But when we surrender fear, hurt, anger, and despair, inner strength is renewed. We know that by the activity of Spirit in and through our lives, all things are working together for our good. We trust that even in the darkest of moments, there remains the promise of impending light. And so it is that in the midst of the deepest desolation, we turn within for solace and direction. Peace is restored once we remember that no matter what manner of trouble is threatening to overtake us, God is with us and we will overcome. It is from within the sanctuary of her deep faith that the awakened woman finds her greatest peace. So, rest easy. Mother. Father. Everything. God's got you!

MEDITATIVE THOUGHT

The Divine Protector is my refuge and my strength.
No matter what comes, my faith abides.

WISDOM PROTOCOL

Recall a trial you've already overcome. Write a journal entry describing how the experience strengthened your faith. List the ways in which divine love was expressed through the kindness of others. Keep the list in a safe place, and review it whenever you're feeling doubtful or frightened about a life experience that you face.

CHAPTER 29

Tomorrow Becomes Yesterday

Resistance is the secret of joy.

—ALICE WALKER

Among the items in my memorabilia collection is the October 12, 1860, edition of the *Liberator*, a popular abolitionist newspaper of the time. One brief story reads: "Louisa, a slave woman of Gen. Miles of New Orleans, has not only stolen herself but carried off $7,000 worth of her mistress' jewelry." That's right! Decades before Bishop Henry McNeal Turner issued what is considered by historians to be the first public call for reparations during Reconstruction, Louisa was already there in consciousness. Apparently, Louisa had taken stock of her situation and determined that resistance was very necessary. Somewhere within herself she was able to capture a vision of a greater good. Though enslaved, Louisa did not agree that a body should be owned and her services rendered for free. Thus, when she liberated herself, she took what she considered to be a measure of just compensation—an amount which, in today's currency, would equate close to $200,000. In 1860, the average white male general laborer earned about $5.88 for a sixty-hour workweek. So it appears that Louisa's calculations included wages, bonuses, plus pain and suffering! Still, no amount of money could compensate for the daily indignities of slavery. Despite tremendous risk, Louisa exercised personal agency. She was free enough in the sanctuary of her mind to exercise control and act in her own best interest. How effectively do we demonstrate healthy self-agency today?

If you're at all like me, you've become increasingly frustrated with the indolent pace of change in the social justice arena. In too many instances, our tomorrows have become yesterdays that have borne little fruit in resolving the issues of most significant impact. For example, how long have we been having the same conversations about income inequality, under-resourced schools, and health disparities? Yes, I get it. These issues are complex, and resolving them requires dismantling layers of interdependent and overlapping systems of inequity. And yes, creating a world that honors the dignity of each person is protracted work that requires our active engagement for the long haul.

It also requires that a certain mindset be cultivated within those whose purpose is to help bring that world to fruition. Is it just me? Or is anyone else pained by glaring limitations of our existing protest playbook? Something happens, and as a community, we feel violated or outraged. Some of us take to the streets with signs. Others call into talk radio to let the community know that they're "fired up and won't take no more." Blog posts proliferate in cyberspace. A good portion of us stay at home and talk with one another about the latest incident. We phone, write, and visit elected officials to call for meaningful and lasting solutions. For a few days, CNN and other networks consider our cause "Breaking News." And then, the beat goes on as if nothing ever happened—until it happens yet again. *You know exactly what I'm talking about!*

But what happens after the street protests stop? After the story is no longer breaking news? How do we address inequity and take a stand for justice and the greater good in our daily lives?

Now, let me say up front that I don't want to believe that this is true, but sometimes it seems as if our sense of agency has been compromised. It's as if some of us no longer believe in our power to exercise choice and effect change. Do we no longer see ourselves as agents of change, capable of advancing the interests of our community without being directed by the designated messiah of the day? Have our psyches been infiltrated by some type of codified, irrational fear of acting in our own best interest? Are we ready to take a united stand on behalf of the interests of our people? That's what self-agency is all about. It's the operationalization of the belief that you are powerful enough to exercise choice and enact change. I think back to the self-agency that was so consistently demonstrated by my parents, whose choices were often motivated by social activism and moral responsibility. Decisions about everything from where we shopped to where we dined were filtered through the lens of social responsibility.

Whenever we dined at a new restaurant in an area with a sizable Black community, there was a litmus test that had to be passed before we would place our orders. At least one Black person had to be employed there. We'd enter the restaurant and be seated. As we looked over the menu, we would also look around to see if any of our people worked there. Once someone was spotted, we were good to go. We would order and enjoy our meals. But if we did not see at least one Black person working in some capacity, my dad would ask to speak to the manager. Once the manager arrived at the table, the conversation would go something like this: "Sir, we're here to dine in your fine establishment, but we've noticed that we don't see any people like us working here. Do you employ any Black people?" The answer to that question determined whether we stayed or left.

I can't tell you the number of Black folks who were sent out from the kitchen as proof over the years! But whenever the answer wasn't affirmative, my dad would confidently explain, "Well, sir, we make it a practice not to patronize businesses that don't support our community. It wouldn't make sense for us to pour money into an establishment where our people can't even get work. I'm sure you understand." With that said, we'd get up and leave. Often, extended family and friends would be with us. So sometimes we would Blaxit ten to fifteen people deep. There was no animus. No desire to be seen or to make a scene. It was all pleasant and very matter-of-fact. My parents believed in exercising choice in ways that supported the advancement of Black people, and they didn't view it as practical or wise to support businesses that didn't support people like them. Growing up, experiences like this happened frequently enough that it was very normal to me. Exercising self-agency became second nature. Some other time, I'll tell you about money marking and their rules for retail shopping!

We've always resisted. We've resisted injustice, indignity, and inequity on every front. Resistance is an affirmation of psychologically healthy selfhood. It is an outgrowth of the intrinsic belief that every human life is of great value and worthy of just, humane, and equitable treatment. Resistance is the foresight that sears through the stubborn inertia of life as we know it to create a better version of the world. Yet, here in the matrix, acts of resistance are often assigned negative labels to silence voices of dissent and to discourage affiliation. When opponents use labels such as *radicals*, *rabble-rousers*, and *enemy forces* (shout out to the Missouri National Guard) to reference those who are calling out societal contradictions and acting as agents of change, it is nothing new. It's happened to every heroine and hero who has demonstrated the courage to effectively challenge the status quo. These verbal assaults are nothing more than the deathbed whispers of dying paradigms clinging to life. Don't allow this to dissuade you from taking decisive action designed to improve conditions and create a better world.

As women, we play a critical role in creating a strong vision for ourselves and in shaping how our loved ones see themselves in relationship to the world around them. What are we modeling? What are our beloveds learning when they observe us? Do our actions demonstrate self-agency, self-love, and self-respect? Are we modeling critical thinking and discernment in our actions?

Recently I had a conversation with a bright and beautiful young mom named Shaquita, who was complaining about the lack of quality foods offered in her neighborhood market. "Why do you continue to shop there?" I asked. "Because that's really the only store around here," she replied. I pointed to her T-shirt and said, "But you're a Black queen. Doesn't the queen have choices?" I challenged. She shrugged her shoulders.

I said, "If the Queen of Sheba walked into a local market to shop for food for her babies, and the stench of rotten meat greeted her at the door, what would she do?"

Shaquita answered, "She'd turn around and walk out of the store without spending a dime."

"Exactly," I opined. "She'd rebel, and that's exactly what you and any other self-respecting woman should do. Find somewhere else to shop, even if it means a longer drive or bus ride to do so."

She smiled and shared, "Well, I guess I could drive to the other market. Sometimes I just don't feel like driving, but I get it now. I won't shop there anymore."

Shaquita, with some gentle prompting, was wise enough to reclaim a sense of self-agency. Once she was able to channel that queenly consciousness within, her choice was a no-brainer. Of course, she wouldn't support a business that had never valued her or her children enough to offer quality products. That's not radical or subversive; it's common sense. It's self-respect. If our communities were filled with people who possessed Shaquita's wisdom, businesses offering inferior products or services would become obsolete because there would be no customers to sustain them. If the status quo doesn't honor the very best of who you are, love yourself enough to choose something better. Each day we have an opportunity and a responsibility to contribute to the creation of a brighter tomorrow. What will you do today?

MEDITATIVE THOUGHT

My choices shape my reality. I exercise self-agency and act in the best interest of myself, my family, and the community.

WISDOM PROTOCOL

Create a "scratch-off list" and post it on the refrigerator. Whenever you encounter a business that engages in discriminatory practices or provides poor quality goods or services, add them to the list. Choose not to patronize those businesses. As you add companies to your list, make it a teaching moment by discussing the power of self-agency with those living in your household.

CHAPTER 30

About That Twenty

I consider income inequality the most dangerous part of what's going on in the United States.

—ALAN GREENSPAN

The irony of Harriet Tubman's image being selected to adorn the twenty-dollar bill as the economic disparity impacting communities of color persists is too much to ignore. While the gesture of making Harriet the new face of money is nice, it's safe to say that—based on what we know about her life of social activism—she'd encourage us to take the tribute deeper by understanding the actual value of that twenty-dollar bill. Here are three rules we should remember when thinking about that twenty dollars.

Rule #1: *Know your number.* Frequently, equal pay advocates in the United States will remind us that women make only seventy-nine cents for every dollar earned by a man. That's true. But, unless you're a non-Hispanic white woman, that's not your number. The wage gap is far worse for women of color than for other groups. In 2016, Black and Latina women working full-time, year-round, earned sixty-four cents and fifty-six cents, respectively, for every dollar earned by a non-Hispanic white male. *So, Sistahs, that $20 in earnings for a white male is actually about $12.80 (for Black women) and $11.20 (for Latinas)*. Resultantly, Black women work nearly nineteen months to equal what white men earn in twelve months. Over the course of a forty-year career, it is estimated that unequal pay results in income losses of over $800,000 for Black women and over one million dollars for Latina women. The lifetime wage loss for Asian-American women is less, though still inequitable, at approximately $360,000.

The National Committee on Pay Equity projects that, at the current rate, white women will receive equal pay sometime around 2059, far ahead of Black and Hispanic workers of both genders. If the glacial pace of change persists, Black women are expected to achieve pay equity by 2124 and Hispanic women by 2233. That's right, 106 years and 215 years respectively, according to The Status of Women Report, 2015, published by the Institute for Women's Policy Research. Economists attribute the reasons for the pay gap to multiple factors, including that women tend to be employed in jobs and industries that pay less and that women tend to have shorter work tenures. Yet they concede that about 40 percent of the pay discrepancies are due to "unknown" factors, which are likely the result of conscious and unconscious bias. Pay discrimination is detrimental to women of color, our families, and communities.

Rule #2: *Understand what the numbers mean for you and your community*. Black and Latina women are more likely to be primary income earners or significant contributors to family finances. The trickle-down effect of disparate wages and employment practices can be observed across the landscape of our communities. The broad strokes used to paint the national economic narrative seldom reveal the true colors of what's happening in Black and Brown communities.

When the 4.7 percent national unemployment rate was reported in May 2016 by the U.S. Bureau of Labor, the unemployment rate for Black people was 8.2 percent and 5.6 percent for Hispanics. If you reside in a predominantly Black and urban metropolis like Detroit, where the unemployment rate was 9.8 percent at that time, there was even greater variance between the national narrative and your reality. The unemployment numbers for our young people living in major cities are even more abysmal.

Communities of color are disproportionately impacted by poverty. In 2014 the poverty rate in the African-American community (26.2 percent) exceeded that of Hispanics (23.6 percent), Asian-Americans (12.0 percent), and whites (10.1 percent) (Census Bureau report on income, poverty and health insurance coverage, 2014). African-American and Hispanic children under the age of eighteen faced the highest poverty rates at 37.1 percent and 31.9 percent respectively. Regardless of educational attainment, the Black unemployment rate is around double the white unemployment rate. And here's the kicker: As stated in a 2015 report by the Economic Policy Institute, "It is, and always has been." Do you think that economic challenges only affect the poorest among us? If so, think again.

Rule #3: *Understand that systemic and structural impediments affect our communities across the spectrum of class.* In January 2015, the *Washington Post* published a series of articles detailing the impact of the housing crisis on the country's most affluent Black community. Prince George's County, Maryland, is the wealthiest Black majority county in the United States. The subdivision of Fairwood, known for its showcase homes with neatly manicured lawns, once stood as a bastion of Black middle-class success. The fact that the community was built on the grounds of a former slave plantation served as a sort of poetic justice. Fairwood was "the place to be" until the community was flooded by the foreclosure crisis, which left over 50 percent of the homes in Fairwood underwater. What happened in Fairwood was replicated in Black communities across the country.

It has now been documented that Blacks disproportionately received high-interest mortgages, even when their credit scores and other financials should have qualified them for lower interest rate loans. Between 2005 and 2009, the net worth of Black households plunged by 53 percent. The full impact of the decimation of Black wealth resulting from the housing crisis won't be realized for years to come. The exposé on Fairwood also demonstrated a pattern of systemic racism that continues to be revealed through research studies and court proceedings. According to the *Washington Post*, court documents detail lending practices that included incentives for aggressively marketing "ghetto loans" to communities of color. Black women, in particular, were targeted for subprime loans; and upper-income Black women were five times more likely to receive a subprime loan than their upper-income white male counterparts. Over 30 percent of borrowers in Prince George's County with annual incomes more than $200,000 were placed in subprime loans. Can you smell the reeking stench of inequity and exploitation?

While our specific challenges may vary across the lines of class, we each encounter the very tenuous nature of our economic standing on a daily basis. Our collective reality as women of color is that we face numerous systemic and structural constraints that impede our capacity to build and sustain solid financial foundations. Does this sober reality mean that there's no hope for us? Not at all. Knowing and understanding the numbers is a necessary first step in getting an accurate pulse on our financial affairs. But the numbers aren't everything. Once we have decoded the economic narrative, we can begin to formulate and act upon viable solutions. The stakes are too high to bury our heads in the sand. By empowering ourselves with information, we can begin to forge a vibrant, new, economic reality.

MEDITATIVE THOUGHT

I am traveling the pathway to financial freedom and prosperity.

WISDOM PROTOCOL

Make an honest assessment of your financial life and determine if you are in bondage or freedom. If there are ways in which you are in financial bondage, begin planning your escape now by reviewing the following five steps and acting on those that apply to your situation:

1. ***Set a solid financial goal.*** Determine where are you now and where you'd like to be six months from now. Make sure that the financial goal you set is measurable (i.e., "Today, my savings account has a $1,000 balance, and six months from now the balance will be $3,000").
2. ***Identify three actions that you can take to accelerate the time it will take you to eliminate debt*** (i.e., taking a part-time job, temporarily moving to a cheaper apartment, getting a roommate, waiting another year before taking on a new car note and applying those funds to debt elimination).
3. ***Find out how your pay compares to that of others who are performing the same work.*** If you are an employee, initiate the conversation by asking your manager: "Is my current pay rate comparable to that of others in the same role? Where does my pay fall along the continuum?" If you are self-employed, find out if what you are

being compensated for goods and services is equitable to what your counterparts are earning. If you're being undercut, put a plan in place to eliminate the disparity.

4. ***If you are in a position of influence within an organization, encourage greater financial transparency.*** Ask that salary information be disaggregated by race and gender when presented to executive leaders for review. Ensure that the data is analyzed and any disparities called out and addressed.
5. ***Consider more than convenience when determining which financial institutions get to hold your money.*** Institutions that have lots of ATMs but also have a history of predatory *lending* don't deserve your financial fidelity. Do business with institutions that value your patronage and treat you fairly. Don't be afraid to ask hard questions, and do the research necessary to obtain the information needed to make an informed decision.

CHAPTER 31

But Don't You Own Nothing?

God bless the child who's got [her] own.

—BILLIE HOLIDAY

Devon Avenue is a multicultural gem located on the far north side of Chicago. Walking down the street in this Rogers Park community is like being transported to another place and time. An international marketplace comprised of a vast array of ethnic grocery stores, restaurants, and specialty shops line the streets. The succulent scents of East Asian spices waft through the air. The area is sometimes referred to as Little India, but that name doesn't reflect the actual diversity of the neighborhood. If you're looking to rent a Bollywood film, purchase a vibrantly colored sari to wear, or shop for intricately made gold jewelry, you'll find it here. And, if your taste buds brought you out, a seemingly infinite number of Asian, Indian, Jewish,

Middle Eastern, and Pakistani restaurants abound, each promising the best in authentic cuisine.

Visiting Devon Avenue reminds me, in many ways, of the Detroit neighborhood in which I grew up. Black business owners were the drivers of commerce in our community. Sure, there were one or two Jewish merchants who had remained longer than their peers who had fled soon after the 1967 rebellion. We also saw a crop of new merchants of Chaldean descent emerging. Still, almost every good or service needed by someone *in* the community was provided by someone *from* the community. Brother John owned the convenience store on the corner of our block and the apartment building above it. The Browns repaired and shined our shoes in their shoe repair shop. The Glenn family cared for our clothes in their cleaners. Mr. Copeland owned the car wash and the salvage yard a few blocks away. Frenchie's, our local diner, served wholesome meals, breakfast through dinner. The House of Joy was our crown jewel. Wives, mothers, sisters, daughters, and friends rotated through the beautifully appointed and spacious salon like clockwork to get their hair "fried, dyed, and laid to the side." Our family's doctor's office and dentist were located within easy walking distance. My piano teacher lived on the same street and provided lessons in her living room, exactly fifty-two steps down the block. I started counting the steps the same summer I started resenting having to go inside for lessons while everyone else played outside. My parents, unmoved by my pouting and slow-walking ways, thought it was funny. As I meandered down the street, one of them would inevitably help me keep track of time by hollering out, "Baby girl, what step are you on? Your piano lesson starts in thirty seconds!"

It was the late 1970s, over a decade out from the passage of landmark legislation, the Civil Rights Act of 1964. It was years after the uprising left block after block of city streets charred. Years after our Black, shining prince had fallen and our king laid to rest. There were subtle signs of slippage, but we were still holding on strong. In an era when Black was vociferously beautiful, we were a melanated mecca. The Detroit I grew up in was home to the most affluent African-American population in the country. Our parents comprised the largest percentage of homeowners that our tribe had ever known. Big shiny cars, many paid for by Big Three jobs and supplier relationships, ruled the roadways. We even had Mayor Coleman Alexander Young, a brilliant and bold take-no-prisoners-and-Hit-Eight-Mile-Road-if-you-don't-like-how-we're-living Black man, at the helm. The immensely powerful psychological impact of coming of age in a place where the leaders, authority figures, and "movers and shakers" look like you, cannot be denied. The powerful unspoken message it sends is: *People like me do great things. We are builders and leaders.* When excellence is the norm and not the exception, you see yourself and the world around you differently.

No, it wasn't all peachy, in case you're wondering. The decline of the automotive industry and the resulting loss of manufacturing jobs, the economic fallout of the Great Recession, the continuation of white flight, and further deterioration of the city's tax base were among the very real and formidable challenges of that time. Still, life within our beautiful enclave was good and served as a buffer. In fact, some of the magic of that era continues to bless the city today. Mayor Young campaigned on promises to integrate the city's majority white police force and to disband the department's oppressive S.T.R.E.S.S. Unit, a decoy unit made infamous by their antagonistic relationship with the Black community. Mr. Mayor made good on both promises and implemented a community policing approach that served as the forerunner of programs that were subsequently implemented across the nation. The fact that Detroit has not been at the epicenter of any of the recent bevy of national stories about extrajudicial killings by police is arguably rooted in this legacy. Things may not be perfect, but the relationship between the community and the police in Detroit is demonstratively better than in many places across the country. Seeds that were sown all those many years ago continue to bear fruit.

Detroit, during the late seventies and eighties, was a great place to come of age. But over the next decade, something Houdini happened and everything changed. My beloved mecca became almost unrecognizable, save the familiar faces of longtime neighbors who by choice or by force had remained. This couldn't have been what Ella Josephine Baker, Charles Hamilton Houston, and the other architects of the Civil Rights Movement intended as the aftermath of dismantling Jim Crow. Fannie Lou Hamer, Daisy Bates, and Yuri Kochiyama couldn't have dreamed that fifty years later we would become a community known for having more, but owning less. Is it even imaginable that their service and sacrifice were fueled by the belief that we would grow to be a mighty consumer nation? Yes, I certainly do think that they would acknowledge the strides we've made. Most assuredly, they would be proud of our continued legacy of overcoming. Still, after the celebratory tears had been shed, don't you think they'd eventually look at us side-eyed and ask, "But don't you own nothing?"

The promise of integration was that it would create greater access to opportunities that had been historically denied to disenfranchised communities. With opportunity would come upward mobility and greater self-sufficiency. But something went awry. While this noble goal did achieve limited success, it also resulted in unanticipated collateral damage. Our folks left the sanctuary of culturally rich, interdependent, self-sustaining communities and went out to claim bigger pieces of the American pie. We can only imagine what it must have been like for them, the first generations to have legal access to the long-yearned-for "other side of the fence." They ventured out to embrace the full bounty of possibility that awaited them in the land made prosperous on the backs of their people. It made perfect sense that they would rush out to claim their rightful inheritance.

But it turned out that America wasn't as ready as they were. This new ideal of a just, integrated, and equal America was met with old ways of thinking, doing, and being that resulted in uneven adherence to the principle of fair play. The passage of laws, no matter how noble, could not erase the stench of white supremacy that permeated every aspect of society. Integration was a social experiment flawed by its attachment to insidious and interwoven systems of structural inequities that recalibrate as needed to maintain the power imbalance and the status quo.

Flash forward. Here we are—coursing through the first decades of the new millennium—the most educated, quasi-assimilated, and moneyed Black people on the planet. Yet we lack the infrastructure to create jobs and recycle dollars within our own communities. The stratospheric success of the few hasn't offset the lack of parity experienced by the rest of us. We are deficient in land ownership, owning less than 1 percent of the country's land according to the U.S. Department of Agriculture. We seem bereft of the collective consciousness needed to walk lockstep and to leverage what power we do have to secure collective wins. Yes, we've made gains. But we've lost a lot too. It is important to acknowledge progress, but we must work toward achieving economic, social, and political equity.

As women, we have an influential role to play in reshaping the economic narrative in our community. We influence virtually every financial decision made, and many of those decisions rest squarely upon our shoulders. We must begin to inculcate a culture of economic self-sufficiency in our homes, schools, businesses, and religious institutions. And if you're already doing that, how can you help to spread the message even further? What new conversations and behaviors must we initiate to heal the diseases of hyper-consumerism and blithe dependency? Our overall prosperity and the well-being of our community are inextricably linked to our willingness to change course and return to the wise principles and practices passed down to us by our foreparents. The good news is that many of us have already begun to return to their course. If the current trend in business ownership is any indication, we're headed in the right direction!

Women of color are turning the tide on the economic trajectory that has ravished our communities. Over the past eighteen years, the number of businesses owned by Black and Latina women has skyrocketed! Firms owned by Black women grew by an astounding 322 percent, while Latina-owned companies increased by 224 percent. Firms owned by nonminority women grew by 40 percent over the same period of time. Today, over 14 percent of all businesses in the United States are owned and operated by African-American women, contributing over $52 billion in revenue and employing almost 300,000 thousand workers. This is an outstanding start.

As phenomenal as this is, owning a business isn't for everyone, and that's perfectly okay. It's merely one face of ownership. Planting a community garden and engaging young people in the process of seeding, nurturing, and harvesting their own food, is another equally important way of stimulating thought about the importance of self-sufficiency. Investing in the future of your favorite community cultural institution is another means of helping to re-establish collective strength. Buying and developing land is yet another. The areas of opportunity are infinite! Follow the paths that speak to your soul and commit to doing all you can to support the restoration of vibrant communities.

MEDITATIVE THOUGHT

God bless the child who's got her own!

WISDOM PROTOCOL

Spend some time thinking about goods or services you could provide if you needed to do so for economic survival. Would you finally launch that catering business? Or start a chauffeur service? Make a list of business ventures that would make sense for you.

Actively support sisterpreneurs and other business owners who contribute to the economic vitality of the community. It's not enough that we're big spenders. Our superconsumer status won't create jobs or assist us in leveraging our economic might to drive much-needed social and political change. We must own and sustain businesses in order to thrive and build generational wealth.

Determine your Door Number 2. Every woman should have a secure back-up plan. If your primary source of income was eliminated today, what can you do for yourself tomorrow to keep the economic tide flowing in your household? Have you socked away enough savings to live six to eight months worry-free as you explore potential work opportunities? If so, good. If not, what will you do if the corporate well runs dry?

Are you building a real estate empire? Investing in properties that will generate passive income. Any idea how many hours you'd have to drive Uber each week to meet your monthly financial obligations if your regular source of income was suddenly no longer available? Or would leasing a business sedan and hiring a driver to fulfill corporate transportation contracts be more your speed?

Every woman should have a solid plan in place that doesn't place her at the mercy of someone else for survival. Have you kept your cosmetology licensed renewed? Just in case. Figure out your plan B. Even if you never have to use it, you'll feel better knowing you've got a plan.

CHAPTER 32

Learning to Fall

Challenges make you discover things about yourself that you never really knew. They're what make the instrument stretch—what makes you go beyond the norm.

—CICELY TYSON

At some point we all fall. We fall short of achieving a goal. We fall behind on our bills. We fall off the diet. We fall out of love. We fall flat on our faces, just before falling apart. Failure, disappointment, and heartache are as natural as the human heartbeat. On the path to each victory, there are stumbles and crash landings along the way. Over time we become better able to mitigate the impact of the dance with disappointment by buffering ourselves with disciplined spiritual practice. Even then there are times when we're caught off guard. The fall comes so unexpectedly or cavernously that we utterly amaze ourselves by continuing to breathe. There's a certain sweetness and impertinence born from learning to fall: It's called tenacity. There's a power that comes from knowing that no matter what comes your way, you have the *bon courage* to lean into it and align with the tide of life as it brings you safely to shore. The awakened woman no longer fears or disparages the low lands of life because she recognizes them as necessary pit stops on her journey to higher ground. She doesn't confuse temporary destinations with her ultimate destiny. She captures grace in imperfect places and moves on.

One of the biggest misperceptions about spiritual growth is that if your journey is sincere, you won't experience the life upsets that nonsojourners endure. Nothing could be further from the truth. Living a Spirit-filled life doesn't exonerate you from the experiences that are common to humanity. Rather, it empowers and equips you to meet those challenges, come what may, with renewed strength and the assurance that everything will be okay in the end. It's not at all uncommon for those who possess great gifts and great earthly missions to endure significant trials as they are molded into who they must become in order to fulfill their divine purposes. When we understand the character-building attributes of adversity, this makes perfect sense. Those difficult circumstances and challenging people were all part of the unfoldment of the divine plan that molded you into the person of consciousness and character who could fulfill your life's purpose. "Study to show yourself approved" takes on new meaning as an incantation about readiness, not worthiness.

When she became a teen mom at sixteen years old, many predicted that she and her son would become just another statistic. But becoming a mom actually fueled her determination to succeed. Later, when her marriage failed, and the business tanked, some observers thought the end was in sight. Yet this young woman persevered. When she lost her home and was forced to sleep in a sleeping bag and cleanse herself and her son in a public restroom, things looked grim. Still, she remained focused on ensuring that her son was well cared for and that her business would thrive. Today, Cathy Hughes is a bonafide media mogul and inspiration to wise women everywhere. Her multimedia Radio One empire serves as the lifeblood of Black news, culture, politics, and entertainment in urban communities across the United States. The publically traded enterprise is made up of fifty-two stations disbursed over fifteen markets, with total assets estimated to exceed $1.4 billion.

Cathy Hughes is a trailblazer who personifies the characteristics of focus and discipline exemplified by the wise woman sojourner. She is a living, breathing example of what's possible when we hold fast to a higher vision, even when the rumble and tumble of life leaves us feeling pressed and scorned. Did you know that when Cathy Hughes was attempting to raise capital to purchase her first radio station, her loan request was denied thirty-two times by thirty-two different financial institutions? She was finally approved by a female Puerto Rican loan officer at the thirty-third bank that she approached. How would the trajectory of her life, and the lives of those in the community served by Radio One, be different if she'd given up after the tenth, twentieth, or thirtieth denial? What was it within Cathy Hughes that emboldened her to continue moving forward after encountering roadblocks, setbacks, and detours along the way to her destiny? She credits her trust in a higher power!

Today, this wise woman who grew up in the projects of Omaha and who, as a young, divorced mother, cooked soup on a hot plate to feed her son, is a model philanthropist who supports the work of homeless shelters, senior citizen programs, and other noteworthy causes. She has remained true to her activist roots and continuously leveraged the strength of her influence and resources to efforts aimed at uplifting the community. Even though she operates in a sphere of wealth and privilege, she has maintained strong ties to the community. Cathy Hughes exemplifies passionate and purposeful living of the highest order. We can all be inspired by her example! Indeed, we are fortunate to have many strong examples of women who have overcome great odds and went on to achieve great heights in their professions—and we celebrate each one of them. For me, it is Cathy Hughes' status as a single mom that really resonated. As you're aware, a disproportionate number of women of color—especially Black women are single moms. Some are single moms by choice and other by circumstance. Regardless of how a woman became a single mother, the messaging received from the broader society is that embracing motherhood creates limitations that can't be overcome. While single parenting does present its own unique challenges, it doesn't automatically signal the end of the road for women who also seek to experience success and fulfillment in other areas of their lives. Plus, motherhood brings its own immeasurable blessings. Not the least of which is the tremendous inner drive that it produces.

If you're a single mom, don't allow anyone to convince you that some carrot dangled in your face—whether it be fame, wealth or prestige—is of greater value than your role as a mom. You must define for yourself how success will be measured in your life. Hold on to that verve and passion for living that empowers you to build a quality life for yourself and your children. Know that the road that you travel may not be the "traditional" route, but who says it should be? The path to your destiny is as unique as you are. Just keep the faith, continue pressing forward and trust that you're on course to experience the greatest vision for your life.

A woman who has learned to fall views adversity through a different lens. She stands awakened, knowing that its purpose is to teach her and not to defeat her. She is adept at asking questions and living the honest answers required in their wake. Her tenacity fuels her growth. A woman who has learned to fall is a woman who is destined to soar!

MEDITATIVE THOUGHT

Failure is a lesson. Success is that lesson applied.

WISDOM PROTOCOL

Think about three important life lessons that you mastered through an experience of adversity. Write about them in your journal. Reflect on what you discovered about yourself in the process.

CHAPTER 33

Revivify: Who Is He, and What Is He to You?

And if you knew him you would know
why we must honor him.

—OSSIE DAVIS

Each New Year's Day was greeted the same way. My father, C.W., along with our next door neighbors—the male heads of households on both sides of us—would rise early and prepare to make their rounds. The early start was as necessary as the visitations themselves. By 7 a.m., I would hear my father announcing to my mother that he and the men were about to leave. The Davenports lived next door on one side of our family, and the Willingham family lived next door on the other side. They would begin by visiting each of the three family homes.

The men would remove their hats as they entered through the front door of the first home and walk all the way to the back of the house. Warmly, they would extend New Year's greetings and exchange other pleasantries with the family members as they moved through the home. Silently, or with quiet utterances, they extended prayers as they executed their duty. Within ten minutes or so, they would depart and move on to the next home, where the scene would be repeated. After blessing each other's homes, they would get in a car and make rounds to the remaining homes on that year's list. They would visit families in the community where there was a man in the home with whom they shared a close relationship. It was a considered a type of brother-to-brother acknowledgment and courtesy. Those stops were outnumbered by the walk-throughs conducted in homes where no strong male presence existed. Among them were the homes of widows, the elderly or sickly, and single mothers.

These were not social visits. My father and our neighbors were engaged in the practice of ritual, even though it's unlikely that any of them would refer to their actions in that manner. From their perspective, they were simply following the tradition modeled by the men they knew. The First Footing ritual, as I later learned that the practice was called, was practiced in Black communities across the Southern United States. The practice was rooted in the belief that the first person to visit a home in the New Year set the tone for the affairs of that home and family throughout the coming year. Furthermore, it was believed that a man should be the first visitor in order to form a hedge of protection around the family and home. First Footing was a carryover from an era when men were squarely cast in the role of provider and protector, and these were responsibilities that many men in the community took seriously during that time, as Moe and Velda can attest.

THIS IS NOT HOW WE GET DOWN

Moe and Velda were a middle-aged couple who moved into an upper flat across the street from where we lived. They didn't have any children. Moe worked at a factory, and Velda was his stay-at-home, common-law wife. They liked loud music—Millie Jackson and Isaac Hayes, especially. It was also apparent that they were close friends with Seagram's and Jack Daniels. But that's not where the rubber met the road. There was something troubling going on in their household, and folks on the block knew it. Velda had been seen with a black eye on one occasion and with a busted lip on another. When asked about it, she blamed it on the alcohol and denied there was any abuse. Some nights, mostly on Saturdays, after the loud music had been turned down and Moe had stormed out of the house, Velda could be heard crying. A couple of times the police had been seen talking to Moe on the front porch, but he was never taken away. Velda's weekly cry-athons continued. This was very upsetting to everyone who was aware of what was happening. During that time, domestic violence was treated as a personal matter, and perpetrators were not routinely held accountable for their actions by law enforcement. The conversation among the adults was, "This has *got* to stop." Fortunately, it did.

On this particular Saturday night, the usual ruckus happened as Bobby Womack played in the background. Shortly after that, Moe stormed out as usual and left Velda to nurse her bruises and dry her tears until about 3 a.m., long after everyone had turned in for the night. Later, before daybreak, through open windows, a loud, deep moaning and crying noise could be heard coming from Moe and Velda's place. The sound was horrible, like an ailing wildebeest in deep pain. It was Moe! He cried and cried. All. Night. Long.

The next day, word traveled in the neighborhood that Moe had gotten himself into some trouble while he was out the night before. No one seemed to know exactly what happened, but by the time his bloodied and battered body returned home, he was a changed man. Whatever befell Moe that night turned out to be just the "get right' therapy he needed. In the remaining years that the couple continued to live on our block, there was no further indication of violence in their home. Soon after the incident, Velda took a job at the local cleaners, where she earned her own money and was frequently seen by the neighbors. She appeared to be much happier. Moe sobered up. They were both better.

Although the details of what happened that fateful night were never confirmed, rumor had it that Moe had run into some of the other men from the neighborhood. He was called out for "hitting his old lady." An argument ensued. Things escalated after Moe invited the men to "stay the hell" out of his business. The men decided otherwise. Fists were thrown, and poor Moe drew the short end of the stick. No one ever talked about who'd been involved. Nor did anyone express regret over what had happened. Moe wasn't respected or seen as "one of us." There were certainly people who engaged in behaviors that others may have considered unsavory—but a man beating a woman broke code.

It was a very different time. The bonds and sense of shared responsibility that existed within the community were much more substantial than what most of us experience today. My father and his contemporaries brought this Black, southern, cultural custom, First Footing, with them when they moved North and started families. It wasn't just something that they did; it was a representation of who they were. To some, this may appear to have been no more than superfluous superstition. But a closer exploration of the context from which this tradition emerged informs us otherwise.

America's segregated South was steeped in the malignant evil of Jim Crow. Black people existed in a perpetual state of peril. The fibers of Black family life were routinely ripped apart by racism, poverty, and other horrors too numerous to name. It was an era in which domestic terrorism not only existed but was backed by the law of the land. The only sure things that Black people could rely on were the Creator and each other. Individual and collective survival necessitated the preservation of strong communal bonds. Upholding the First Footing ritual was a way of saying, *We see you. We've got you. We're in this together.* It was an act of defiance—an affirmation of the strength embodied in their unity and a reminder of the shared commitment to standing together.

The First Footing ritual was not simply an offering made by the men of the community. The women of the village equally extended themselves by holding a space for the men to express themselves in this way. For the women, it was a way of saying, *Regardless of how the dominant culture may seek to define you, we see you clearly. And we honor the truth of who you are.* It's one thing for men to want to show up as a high priest and king, and another for women to create a context where the attributes required to fulfill those roles can be consistently cultivated. Not once did I hear any woman from the community speak disparagingly about the practice. These women were smart, independent thinkers. Most of them worked outside of the home. They were well read and well traveled, yet they didn't express any angst or sense of resentment about participation in the ritual. Rather, the First Footing visits and what they represented were warmly welcomed year after year.

Thinking back on this practice makes me wonder how a First Footing ritual would be received in our community today. Would the presence of men standing up and taking on the role of protectors be welcomed, or viewed as unnecessary? Or, worse, as an unwelcomed imposition? Would the idea of men fulfilling this role be perceived as antiquated, too old-fashioned to be of any contemporary good? Looking at the violence and fragility that plague many of our communities, it stands to reason that the intention behind First Footing, if not the practice itself, is much needed.

Are we, modern-day and modern-ways women, as adept as our mothers at creating contexts that support our men in cultivating spiritual muscles? We are always teaching people how to treat us and how to show up for us. We do so even when we are not consciously aware of what we are calling forth. Are there any ways in which we unwittingly reinforce undesirable behaviors? Examine this and related questions by completing the following Wisdom Protocol.

MEDITATIVE THOUGHT

In unity there is strength.

WISDOM PROTOCOL

In what ways do gender roles in contemporary relationships between women and men differ from those embodied by our foreparents? Are these differences positive or negative? Are there any elements of traditional relationships that should be restored? Which aspects should we let go of for good?

CHAPTER 34

A Note to You

The way to right wrongs is to turn the light of truth on them.

—IDA B. WELLS BARNETT

When I wrote the essay that follows, *Somebody Just Ought to Tell the Truth*, the landslide of sexual misconduct allegations raging through Hollywood, the U.S. Congress, and various media outlets had not yet begun. This heightened level of public discourse about the abusive conditions that women endure in the workplace had long been hoped for by many but was not yet a manifested reality. The spotlight being given to this issue is certainly welcomed, but also vastly incomplete. Although the #MeToo movement was launched by a brave Black woman—activist Tarana Burke—the mass reckonings for sexual misconduct that we're witnessing have primarily been the stories of accusations made against powerful white men by white women of means. Of course there have been a few notable exceptions, but on the whole, the voices of women of color and poor women remain conspicuously absent.

The silence—and the silencing of the most vulnerable women among us—is nothing new. For some women silence is imposed as a survival strategy, the lesser evil in circumstances where speaking out would likely carry consequences more grave than they dare to bear. Consider, for instance, the plight of the low-skilled, low-wage worker who is a single mother and the sole economic provider for her family. What indignities might she suffer in order to feed and clothe her babies? Imagine the undocumented migrant worker who has crossed the border to flee violence and seek refuge for herself and her children—only to find that new forms of violence await her as she endeavors to broker some small measure of peace for her family. Difficult circumstances—and the lack of support systems to successfully mitigate them—induce silence for many women.

What about the women who, despite the risk, do report their tormentors, only to be ignored—or worse, not even believed? Our sisters who are most vulnerable to abuse are also bereft of the power and privilege needed to ensure that their voices would be heard and their concerns acted upon. This reality was poignantly illustrated in a *Ms. Magazine* article authored by Chandra Bozelko that focused on the relationship between sexual abuse, crime, incarceration, and continued abuse in prison. Ms. Bozelko writes:

> *Eighty-six percent of jailed women surveyed in the Vera Institute study reported a history of sexual victimization. According to the Illinois study released last month, 98 percent of the state's female prison population experienced physical abuse, 75 percent had been sexually abused and 85 percent had been emotionally abused. Abuse is a better predictor of incarceration than race (64 percent), than socioeconomic status as measured through employment (60 percent), or than educational attainment measured by having earned a high*

school diploma (37 percent)—the usual co-conspirators who take women down.

Here's the deal. Every woman, regardless of race or socio economic class, deserves to live free from sexual, emotional, and physical abuse. All of our spaces must reflect our belief in this ideal. In order to bridge the gap between the grandeur of our collective aspirations and the ignobility of our shared reality, we must each invest in creating homes, communities, and workplaces where women are valued and respected. We must insist upon sweeping systemic reforms that will drive and sustain new cultural norms that affirm and protect the rights of women. And, we must lead the charge to create them. Until institutional policies and practices align with the goodwill expressed verbally, we remain vulnerable. Without increased transparency and swift accountability, those who act against the best interests of women will continue to hide behind the cloak and shield of power and privilege. There's work for each of us to do. How will you leverage your time, talents, or treasures in support of these aims? It only takes one spark of change to inflame the passions of many. How will you contribute?

CHAPTER 35

Somebody Just Ought to Tell the Truth

Find your own voice and use it; use your own voice and find it.

—JAYNE CORTEZ

It's not okay when an adult in a position of power or authority leverages that position to emotionally or sexually abuse children, teens, or anyone else. It's not okay that we've become immune to the sounds of gunshots and no longer feel or feign surprise when we hear that another schoolchild has been gunned down. It's not okay that our elders no longer feel safe in the communities built on the backs of their sacrifices. It's not okay that corruption has become so commonplace that we both expect and accept it. It's not okay that in some of our homes people we love are being victimized by those we fear while we pretend not to see it happening. And it's not okay that we walk around trying to pretend we don't know that this is not okay. *Somebody just ought to tell the truth about something!*

The sound of our silence is suffocating, and I don't know about you, but some days I can barely breathe. The echo of our collective pain is so loud that it takes my breath away. I just can't do it anymore. I can't worry about offending. I can no longer be bothered with pretending. I can't even fear being misunderstood. Truth must find sanctuary on my tongue and pass safely into the world. When your heart awakens, the gift and the curse is that you see. No longer blinded by the Technicolor façade of worldly living, you see beneath the veil. You see both what is and what could be. You are driven not by the fear of the horrors that you see and speak about, but by the insistence of the higher possibilities desiring to be brought into existence.

The next time that someone tries to tell you that looking away from the pain and injustice present in the world is the best way to eradicate their existence, share these numbers: 10,000 people murdered each day, 400 every hour, 7 every minute as the world watched in unconscionable silence. In 1994, in a span of 100 days, the lives of over one million innocent women, men, and children were taken during a mass slaughter during the civil war in Rwanda. Over 95,000 children were orphaned. Not one world superpower came to their aid. The Tutsi people cried genocide, and the world remained reprehensibly silent. Self-professed "good people" everywhere who remain silent in the face of injustice and wrongdoing should seriously check the accuracy of their moral compass.

Some time ago, I read about the inspiring life journey of human rights activist, Jacqueline Murekatete who was only nine years old when the Hutu-led genocide against the Tutsi in Rwanda occurred. Her parents, her six siblings, and most of her extended family were lost during the violent, machete-laden rampage. Jacqueline and her grandmother, whom she was visiting in another village, initially escaped by taking cover with family and friends. Later they hid at an orphanage, where her grandmother was killed soon after their arrival. The next year Jacqueline was granted asylum and brought to the United States to be reared by her uncle. In the twenty plus years since this horrific tragedy took place, Jacqueline has become an outspoken peace and justice advocate. Today, she serves as the founder and president of the Genocide Survivors Foundation, a New York-based nonprofit organization. She and her team work to educate the public about the crime of genocide and to raise funds to support genocide survivors.

Jacqueline stands as such an excellent example of the resilient nature of the human spirit. She has borne witness to unthinkable horrors and emerged with her humanity intact. She has endured unimaginable loss yet held on to a compassionate heart. Through her activism she confronts hate, challenges indifference, and continues to change hearts and minds. Jacqueline offers the following words of wisdom: "I strongly believe that a more peaceful and equitable world is possible. But it will require the involvement of each and every one of us. So don't be silent, don't stand by—take action."

Silence is no longer golden once you awaken to your power to be a force for good. When righteousness, justice, and peace beg for you to cry out on their behalf, you become an agent of change. Oh, they may not be expecting it, and they may not want to hear it, but pledge to speak truth today about something that matters. Begin by unearthing spaces in your immediate environment where the elixir of truth is needed. Is there any aspect of your family, community or work life where your voice of wisdom is needed? Do not allow fear, ambition or unhealthy levels of needing to be liked to undermine your courage and integrity. Degeneracy looms in the shadows of our silence. Wise woman, speak.

MEDITATIVE THOUGHT

I am a courageous truth-teller.

WISDOM PROTOCOL

Reflect on what's happening in the world around you. This reflection should include the sphere of your personal affairs. What do you observe that seems to be spiraling out of control? Around which issues do you hear people saying, "This has got to stop," yet the problem persists? Most importantly, what would you like to see happen differently? Consider the steps you can take, individually or collaboratively, to make a positive difference. Take action and then reflect on how it feels to give voice to your power.

CHAPTER 36

The Night Has a Thousand Eyes

Don't jump to conclusions—there may be a perfectly good explanation for what you just saw.

—PROVERBS 25:8

Stargazing is one of my favorite pastimes. Since I live in a major city, full of blinding lights, catching a clear view of the night sky requires some effort. Fortunately, several locations within driving distance offer an unfettered view of nature's magnificent night show. One of the first things you notice while stargazing is the sheer magnitude of stars that are present—appreciably more than light-polluted city skies ever reveal. Stars blanket the sky, each one unique and offering its own degree of luminosity. While sitting there and taking in this natural wonder, you experience a keen awareness of your own duality. On the one hand, you are reminded of your minuteness, and on the other, of your inextricable connection to the magnanimity of the universe and all that is. My dark-sky companions have also come to serve as a metaphor for an important lesson about the importance of understanding the limits of human perception.

The night has a thousand eyes. As we travel through life and pursue the fulfillment of purpose, wise women are mindful of their place in the grand scheme of things. We are aware that our perspectives, no matter how cherished and well developed, represent *a way,* but not *the only way* of seeing things. We honor that each path is as unique as the woman who walks it and that policing another woman's journey is not our right, role, or responsibility. We resist entanglement in such delusions of grandeur and devote our attention to lighting up our own piece of the sky and watching in awesome wonder as other women do the same.

EVERYTHING'S NOT WHAT IT SEEMS

Last summer, I watched a father very harshly scold his young son for running out into the street to retrieve a ball. He yelled angrily at the child and dragged him by his little arm back to the sidewalk in front of their home. It was a wonder that the boy's arm didn't pop out of the socket. As a mom, I certainly understood the importance of correcting the child's dangerous behavior, but the intensity of the dad's reaction was way over-the-top. I was observing the interaction from the porch of a house across the street while waiting for my friend to open the door. When she let me in, I was still serving up sistah-glare—a most serious form of side-eye—to the monster dad across the street. Immediately, I asked her, "What's up with your neighbor? He's wailing on that kid like some kind of maniac!" She listened as I recounted what had just happened and replied, "Oh, they'll be fine. Jeremy is a great dad."

She went on to explain that just the day before, the little boy had run into the street and was almost hit by a car. The car screeched to a stop, just millimeters from taking the boy's life. The boy's dad had dashed to stop him but couldn't catch him in time. After cradling his terrified son and then passing him to his mother, the dad sat on the curb and wept openly—horrified by having come so close to losing the love of his life, and overwhelmed with gratitude that his son's life had been spared. In a matter of minutes, I'd gone from feeling upset at what appeared to be the mistreatment of a child, to feeling tremendous empathy for the father, the trauma he had recently endured, and the potential tragedy he had tried to prevent. I went from wondering if he was a fit parent to wanting to run over to Target and purchase one of those leashes that other people put on their children to give him as an apology gift. More importantly, I was reminded of the perils of jumping to conclusions. Here are a few tips on how to avoid leaping before you really look into situations.

Talk to the person directly. If you are genuinely concerned about a perceived issue or a rumor that is circulating about someone, go straight to that person and initiate an authentic conversation. Most people will welcome the dialogue if approached with candor and honesty and without ulterior motive. Begin by stating your intentions and seeking agreement to talk. For example: "I'm concerned about something I'm hearing, and I'd like to discuss it with you. Is that okay?" If the person expresses willingness, approach the conversation with careful words and a compassionate heart. You're not there to stir the pot! If the person doesn't wish to engage in the discussion, for whatever reasons, respect the boundary that has been set and leave it alone. You'll find that most people will discuss just about anything if approached sincerely and respectfully.

Ask. Don't assume or accuse. Sometimes a question is all that's needed to prevent innuendo and misinformation from proliferating. Your words don't have to be profound. A simple and sincere "What's going on?" will do. Some people formulate assumptions based on hearsay and fail to conduct any level of meaningful inquiry into the veracity of what they've been told. They treat second-, third-, and thirty-hand hearsay as if it were firsthand information. This is a most onerous expression of erroneous thinking. We are each entitled to our own opinions, but not to our own facts. If you care enough to have an opinion, care enough to seek the truth. Otherwise, just stay out of it altogether. Whenever accusations are brought to any human interaction, you all but guarantee that defenses will rise and the ability to hear and be heard will significantly diminish. Accusations place the accuser and the accused at odds from the very beginning. Blind accusations leave no room for the exploration of truth or the application of justice. Unless you're operating from firsthand knowledge, avoid accusations altogether. And remember: Even if you think you know what happened, you may not know why it occurred.

Questions—not accusations—offer the most viable pathway to understanding. A relationship that isn't worth a question is a relationship that isn't worth your time. Right? Because if the person or relationship were of value *to you*, asking a question would be a tiny gesture to offer before making assumptions or casting accusations. Likewise, when someone values their relationship *with you*, that person will come to you with any concerns, seeking clarification rather than accepting gossip and innuendo as truth. Sometimes people don't ask questions because they really don't want the truth. They simply attach to the version of the narrative that best satisfies their inner needs.

Don't be blinded by emotions. When our emotions run high, we are more vulnerable to jumping to conclusions. Intense feelings often override rational thought—and for good reason. Emotions stem from a part of our brains that responds more quickly. The emotional centers in the brain are much more like a rocket, in contrast to the rational center of the brain, which operates more like an ascended jet in steady flight. When our emotions are triggered, there's no slow climb, followed by an announcement of having reached a comfortable cruising altitude. No, when our emotions are turned up, we blast off! Truth can become obscured when situations are approached with heavy emotions still at play.

So how do we slow down and become less reactive? Step away from the situation and compose yourself before engaging in conversation about what's going on. Give yourself time to regroup. Once you are feeling more centered and in command of your emotions, begin to initiate a meaningful conversation about the situation at hand. As we grow in wisdom, we are able to ride the highs and lows of life without losing our emotional center. We become more proficient in mastering those parts of our personalities that tend to be more reactive than responsive. More bombastic than balanced. More ego-driven than heart-centered. Thus, we endeavor to be fully present to the emotions that we feel *and* to effectively manage our responses while in the throes of their might.

Own up to your behavior. If people put as much effort into doing right as they do into avoiding the admission of wrong, the world would be a better place. Our spheres of affairs are better when we woman up. One of the most effective ways to discipline oneself to refrain from repeating undesirable behaviors is to commit to correcting missteps as they occur. In this case, that would mean acknowledging when we've jumped to conclusions about someone or something. Owning up to being wrong is an important first step, but in those instances where we have misspoken or mistreated someone based on faulty conclusions, stopping there isn't sufficient. We must acknowledge our error to whoever was adversely influenced or impacted by our words or behaviors.

Resistance to owning our wrongdoing is often rooted in cognitive dissonance: the intense mental stress caused when new information is presented that contradicts an existing belief or firmly held opinion. The ego will often fight mightily to deny the veracity of the new data to ward off self-incrimination. It says to itself, "Well, I don't know if I believe that. It just couldn't be true." It's an attempt to avoid facing an ugly and rabid part of the unhealed self. After all, if you've jumped to conclusions and acted on faulty information, what does that say about you? Whenever someone positions herself as judge, jury, and executioner, it's an indication that the ego has run amok. Thinking too much of yourself and too little of others is a vainglorious flaw that inevitably leads to peril. Getting in the habit of literally walking back missteps fosters increased self-awareness and cultivates a spirit of humility that will impede the impulse to repeat the same behavior. After sitting at the table a few times and tasting the sourness of humble pie, the desire for additional helpings decreases exponentially.

Again: The night has a thousand eyes. We are all confronted by situations that carry more complexity than may be immediately apparent. Although we are sometimes privy to great glimmers of insight, we do not possess the omniscience of the Divine. Whenever we act as if we do, we do a disservice to ourselves and others. Integrate the tips above into your personal toolkit and practice using them to remain grounded when circumstances threaten to take you off center.

MEDITATIVE THOUGHT

There's always more to a story than what meets the eye—and I'm wise enough to know it.

WISDOM PROTOCOL

Reflect on a time when you jumped to conclusions about someone or something, or when you were jumped by someone else's rush to judgment. In hindsight, what did you learn from the situation, and in what ways were you changed by the experience?

Note: "The Night Has a Thousand Eyes" is the title of a famous jazz standard inspired by a poem written by British poet Francis William Bourdillon. My favorite rendition is performed by John Coltrane. It's a lovely tune that you can check out online if you're curious about how it sounds.

CHAPTER 37

Everyday Philanthropy

I have found that among its other benefits,
giving liberates the soul of the giver.
—MAYA ANGELOU

Each day when you arise, set your heart on giving something of value to someone other than yourself. Giving can take on many forms—some remunerative and some not. Maybe it will be your smile that affirms another, your words that help to heal a broken heart, or your act of kindness that restores someone's faith in humanity. It could be your phone call that unexpectedly opens the door of opportunity for someone or your forgiveness that nullifies the memory of a shared and painful past. The capacity to give isn't dictated by financial circumstances or the number of one's possessions. There are infinite ways to make an impact through giving. Familial, community and communal giving are three readily available portals through which philanthropy can be expressed. It all begins with holding a sincere intention. If you're serious about becoming an excellent giver, simply ask: "Beloved Spirit, how shall I give today?"

FAMILIAL GIVING

My first lessons in generosity came from my parents, who approached giving as a way of life. Visitors from near and far were warmly welcomed into my parents' home. Relatives, friends, and friends of friends often found their way to our doorstep. If someone stopped by near dinnertime, they were welcomed to join us at the table. Out-of-town guests received extra helpings of niceties. Bright smiles, sun-bleached linens, home-cooked meals, and warm hospitality were staples. Even when guests showed up unexpectedly and stayed too long, they were made to feel at home. Fortunately, most guests were considerate enough not to impose themselves in those ways.

Friday evenings were especially delightful. Around six o'clock, as I played outside with my friends, the aroma of fried chicken, hot fish, and buttermilk biscuits would billow out from my mom's kitchen window and fill our street. Sometimes I'd be sent to Brother John's, the convenience store on the corner of our block, to pick up condiments or extra napkins before the guests arrived. By seven o'clock, the regulars would start to appear, each familiar face pausing to greet me before crossing the threshold of our front door. By eight o'clock, the entire crew had assembled and the games had begun. The teams would launch into a night of "running Bostons," "smelling the tea," and admonishing the losing team to "rise and fly." Their boisterous laughter and smack-talking would continue long past my bedtime. These gatherings, and others like them, taught me that good hospitality was a form of generosity—and that whatever you have, no matter how humble or grand, was to be shared with those you love. Are you giving of yourself in ways that let those closest to you know just how precious they are?

COMMUNITY GIVING

Community giving was commonly practiced in our neighborhood. These efforts were primarily led by women. Mrs. Smith organized the annual spring planting at the playground on LaSalle. Each year we enjoyed a breathtakingly beautiful garden that she carefully tended on our behalf after the planting was complete. Mrs. Sinclair organized the fall harvest party. Though she didn't have children of her own, each year she would host a gathering for all of the young people in the immediate area. We would meet at her home to enjoy music, food, and games including apple bobbing. Yeah, things were different then. Today the idea of apple bobbing with a group of acne-prone adolescents strikes me as a bit gross too. But back in the day, it was pure, unadulterated fun.

Not so long ago, I came across a stack of newspaper articles my mom had saved. Several of the clippings documented a favorite service activity from my youth: the visit to the senior home. Each year my mom and our neighbors (Mrs. Robinson, Mrs. Davenport, Mrs. Willingham, Mrs. Patton, Mrs. Thompson, Miss Bea and others) led the effort to prepare and distribute care packages at the senior home a few blocks from where we lived. The gift packages consisted of "essentials" such as socks, deodorant, toothpaste, and an array of other toiletry and self-care items. There were enough male and female packages prepared to ensure that each person received a gender-appropriate gift. Each gift was neatly wrapped in holiday-themed paper and a matching bow.

These early lessons about the importance of service—taught by my parents and the Mamas and Babas in our community—left an indelible impression on me. Riding on the strength of their example, I've been engaged in some form of community service throughout my adult life.

COMMUNAL GIVING

Do you remember sou-sous? There was a time when these collective savings clubs were fairly commonplace in African, African-American, and Caribbean communities across the United States. Other communities of color use different names, but the core principles are the same. Sou-sous are formed when a group of people come together and decide to save money and distribute it communally. Let's say that a group of ten women agree to establish a sou-sou and determine that the monthly contribution will be $200 per person. Each month, the $2,000 collected would be given to one woman in the group. This would be repeated each month until every woman received the full kitty at least once. Then the process would begin again. Why, you may be wondering, wouldn't people just save the money on their own since they're not gaining any additional funds by participating in communal savings?

Therein lies the beauty of the sou-sou, whose formation is about much more than money. Sou-sous are an expression of the shared intention to support one another through acts of intragroup self-sufficiency. The communities in which sou-sous formed were those that were most often denied fair access to mainstream financial opportunities. If money was needed for a down payment on a home, to cover school expenses, or to fund a trip back home, the community was a more viable source of support than the financial institution on Main Street. Sou-sous existed on foundations of trust and accountability. Given what the data shows about the persistent pattern of disparate treatment communities of color receive when dealing with major financial institutions, I wonder if intracommunity economic programs will once again emerge? Imagine what would be possible if we adapted these models and took on the challenge of pooling our resources.

Consider how lives would be transformed if 10 percent of the tithes collected at the churches, mosques, and temples in our community were set aside to fund microfinancing programs for community members. How much could we reduce student loan debt among our college-bound young people if they received interest-free tuition loans from the community instead of being reliant on student loan programs that keep them in bondage through much of their young adulthood? Do you realize what a dent we could make in youth unemployment if the members of our organizations and institutions committed to donating one dollar per week, for an entire year, to fund 10-week summer apprenticeship programs? A group of 100 donors could fund the employment of 2 young people for 20 hours per week at $10.50 per hour. Every 1000 donors could put 25 young people to work learning valuable skills. All for only a dollar per week!

Much ado is made about the fact that the African-American community boasts $1 trillion in buying power. Yet when you ride through our communities, the dearth of Black-owned grocery stores, hospitals, financial institutions, communications outlets, manufacturing and distribution facilities, and other means of commerce are glaringly absent. What gives? Can anyone name a single group of people on the planet who have survived and thrived while being economically dependent on others?

FROM THIS MOMENT ON

Maybe you're reading this and thinking, *Wow, I really haven't been a good giver!* You may be wondering if it's too late to turn the corner and reveal the part of yourself that joyously contributes to others. The good news is that it's never too late. Some people spend an entire lifetime giving little to anyone other than themselves. Others are too consumed with receiving to notice any need or opportunity to give within their field of vision. These souls suffer a profound poverty, no matter how much money they make or take. A low balance in your bank account can be quickly overcome. Healing an impoverished spirit requires a much more potent remedy. Sow into someone else's dreams without any expectation that doing so renders that person beholden to you. Show up as the answer to someone's prayer simply because you can. Make refreshing others a part of your personal mission, and watch how blessings begin to chase you down and overcome you!

THE WISE GIVER

Apply wisdom and seek discernment in your giving. Some people will see your generosity as something to be exploited and try to play you! Where to give, when to give, and how much to give are decisions that should be made within the sanctuary of your heart. You have nothing to prove to anyone. Giving is first and foremost a spiritual exercise. Seek guidance on how best to contribute, and follow that direction without apology or explanation. Don't hesitate to deliver a firm *no* to anyone who attempts to manipulate or exploit your generosity.

During a recent lunch conversation with friends, Marisol shared the frustration she feels when her extended family members treat her like "a well-heeled ATM." Marisol is in a position that many successful women find themselves. She's the one in her family who "made it big," at least comparatively. And because her financial wherewithal exceeds that of many of her loved ones, a few relatives have attempted to position her as their "go-to" personal financier. Marisol explains, "Don't get me wrong: I don't mind helping out when a legitimate need arises. When my niece was laid off unexpectedly, I gladly covered her rent for a couple of months to help out. But when she came back a few months later asking for money after she'd quit her new job because her supervisor 'had a bad attitude,' I flat out refused to give her a dime." Marisol's niece was furious that her request for cash was denied and resorted to calling her aunt "selfish" and "uppity." The table erupted in laughter! We'd each lived our own versions of similar money tales with similarly harrowing characters. Marisol remained firm and did not enable her niece's poor decision-making. In refusing her niece's request, she was also modeling wise giving and savvy financial stewardship.

Honor the alchemy of giving. When you give, freely and without expectation, you set into motion universal laws that place a cover of provision over you and yours. Don't wait until you feel that you have enough—because you already do. If you're alive, awake, and aware, you have all that you need to be a vessel for the outpouring of generosity. Determine that from this moment on, you will be a good and wise giver!

MEDITATIVE THOUGHT

I freely and wisely give from the deep well of abundance within me.

WISDOM PROTOCOL

Initiate a conversation with a group of family, friends, or community members about the type of philanthropic footprint you'd like to make. Continue to gather and brainstorm ideas until a plan is in place that you're each working to actualize.

CHAPTER 38

The Beautiful Possible

It is never too late to go quietly to our lakes, rivers, oceans,
even our small streams, and say to the
sea gulls, the great blue herons,
the bald eagles, the salmon, that we are sorry.

—BRENDA PETERSON

Who would have imagined that an entire U.S. city could be ravished by lead-infested drinking water? But, that's exactly what happened in Flint, Michigan, where the drinking water was contaminated beginning in 2014 after a state-appointed emergency manager switched the city's water supply from treated Lake Huron and Detroit River sources to the highly polluted Flint River. Some contend that state regulators failed to mandate that the necessary corrosion control agents be applied to the Flint River source. Drinking water flowed through webs of aging lead pipes and was contaminated as a result. Adding the anticorrosive elements to the water would have cost approximately $100 for three months. Others assert that corrosion agents were used, but that the high levels of chloride in the Flint River make it difficult to sanitize. What we know for sure is that not enough was done to prevent the contaminated water from reaching Flint citizens. Switching the water source was done in an effort to save approximately five million dollars over a two-year period. At the peak of the crisis, the levels of heavy metal measured in the city's drinking water rose above the threshold for hazardous waste. This government-induced public health disaster will have a devastating impact upon Flint's citizens, especially the most vulnerable, for the duration of their lifetimes.

It's been estimated that this man-made calamity has resulted in more than twelve thousand children being chronically exposed to unsafe concentrations of lead. Experts caution that the actual number of impacted children could be far higher because many may have been tested after the lead was no longer detectable in their systems. Decades of scientific studies have documented the adverse impact of elevated blood lead levels. Lead poisoning impacts the part of the brain that controls impulses and emotions, and childhood lead poisoning is correlated with a higher risk for shortened attention spans, behavioral disorders, and intellectual disabilities. What will this mean for the future of Flint's children?

The moms and dads in Flint knew something was wrong with the water long before city and state officials acknowledged their concerns. The tap water was brown and carried a foul smell. Their babies were breaking out in rashes after bathing. The brilliant and courageous pediatrician and public health advocate, Dr. Mona Hanna-Attisha, sounded the alarm and provided empirical evidence that children in Flint were being exposed to dangerous levels of lead. Their concerns were dismissed. Instead, they were told "Go ahead and drink up. We're good". Warnings from the Environmental Protection Agency (EPA) about toxicity levels were also downplayed. It must be noted, however, that as these elected officials looked away from the looming problem in front of them, employees at the State Office Building were being supplied with purified water because officials knew the tap water was not safe. Officials took no decisive action on behalf of the city's residents until increasing public scrutiny forced them to do so. Someone sat in an office and did the math. Someone determined that the price of water safety for Flint residents wasn't worth the cost. Someone decided that Flint lives didn't matter. A report issued by The Michigan Civil Rights Commission concluded, "deeply embedded institutional, systemic and historical racism" contributed to the decisions that resulted in the water crisis. Former U.S. Senator Don Riegle powerfully articulated the sentiments of many in an article that he penned for the Huffington Post: "What has happened in Flint by State Government fiat was madness; and the abject failure to now fully remedy the problem is a monstrous dereliction of duty."

It's been over three years, and the water crisis in Flint has not yet been resolved. Recently, a crippling bacterial infection, shigellosis, spread through the community because residents are too afraid to wash their bodies with water from the contaminated local system and are using free baby wipes distributed by local rescue centers instead. A spike in the number of Legionnaire's disease, resulting in at least 14 deaths, has been linked to the crisis. To date, there have been four resignations, four firings, five suspensions and fifteen criminal indictments. The most serious—involuntary manslaughter—is a 15-year felony charge. Michigan Governor Rick Snyder remains in office. The awfulness of what's happening in Flint has captured the world's attention, but her citizens are not alone. It's estimated that more than 5,000 U.S. water systems are in violation of the Environmental Protection Agency lead and copper rule. Do you know the quality of the water flowing through your tap?

While lamenting over the confluence of bad decisions that resulted in the Flint tragedy, I began to think about how the response to this crisis might play out differently if our collective appetite for concern lasts longer than the most recent news cycle and we responded by taking action on the words that we pray when we intone, "Thy kingdom come, Thy will be done on earth as it is in heaven." Those words aren't intended to be an idyllic abstraction, they're our call to action. What if something beautiful and extraordinary were to blossom out of the painful reality that endures in Flint?

Imagine what would happen if the nation's top health care, educational, spiritual, civic, nonprofit, and business leaders were to combine forces and partner with the community in Flint to transform the city into an epicenter of innovative wraparound community redevelopment programming? The city, with a population of just under one hundred thousand, is right-sized to serve as a demonstration site for innovative practices in each of the aforementioned areas. Flint, with nearly 40 percent of her residents living in poverty, is the perfect place to bring to bear the decades of best practice research on how to effectively support vulnerable communities in redesigning their futures. Lessons learned from the models implemented in Flint could then be brought to scale in other communities grappling with the same issues. Environmental racism, poverty, crime, inadequate nutrition, and under-resourced schools are strangling the life out of far too many communities across this land. How powerful would it be a generation from now, when the children of Flint have reached adulthood, to see them stand before the world and bear witness to the miracles that were created when an awakened world saw their pain and came to their aid. Sure, the prognosis seems bleak today—but that narrative won't remain true unless we fail to bring our collective genius to bear.

Still think that the call for environmental justice doesn't have anything to do with you? Concern for the environment and the right use of natural resources isn't a middle-class, yuppie project du jour. More than the tree huggers have a stake in this game. We each have a place in this work; it's our collective call to action. Together, as we become more ethical about our consumption and more intentional about achieving environmental equity, we will effectively put the brakes on our downward spiral. We, and the generations that will follow us, deserve to enjoy the earth and the fullness of her sweet bounty. But we've got to be smart about it, and we must play fair. If we put off until tomorrow the work that calls forth our hands today, enjoying her riches simply won't be an option. Let's not continue along this path of withholding good from ourselves and from one another. Instead, let's marshal forces and turn the tide. *Swoosh!*

MEDITATIVE THOUGHT

I honor my planetary mother and do my part to restore her to wholeness.

WISDOM PROTOCOL

Identify one thing you will ***start*** doing to support sustainable living for yourself, your loved ones, and the broader community. Identify one thing you will ***stop*** doing because you recognize its harmful impact.

CHAPTER 39

Outro: Celebrating Your Divine Splendor

It was when she recognized her own splendor
that the world told her that she was beautiful.

—UNKNOWN

A GOOD LANDING

Congratulations! We've covered a lot of ground together. You've called forth the wise woman within and followed her lead to greater insights about yourself and the attributes of purposeful living. You've explored the importance of release and the necessity of restoration as precursors to reawakening. You've focused on achieving mastery of your thoughts and actions as a function of your devotion to purpose. You know why you're here. You are an individualized expression of the Most High. You are here to experience the unfoldment of your consciousness so that the Spirit of God can be expressed through you.

You've also made great strides in understanding activism, or sacred service, as a pathway to more purposeful living. As you continue to experience and express more and more of your authentic self, your openness to divine guidance about the best use of your time, talents, and gifts will flourish. You will find ever-increasing value and meaning in living from the core of your being, instead of simply reacting to the insistent demands of the human ego and outer world.

You've cultivated greater intimacy with your inner wisdom and have begun to magnetize the purity, peace, gentleness, openness to reason, mercy and good fruits, impartiality and sincerity of *the wisdom from above* in the world of your affairs. There's definitely reason to celebrate!

Fortunately, the journey doesn't end here. There are an infinite number of rooms in the mansion of spiritual unfoldment awaiting your exploration. Awakening is now your way of life. The awakened life is an inspired life, and it marks a new set point in the ongoing evolution of your consciousness. Here are a few thoughts to keep close at heart as your wisdom journey continues.

THE GREATEST INVESTMENT YOU'LL EVER MAKE

The time, energy, and tears you invest in designing a life that you are passionate about living are the greatest investments you'll make in this lifetime. The strides you make in this area will shape all that you do and become. Don't allow any temporary discomfort to cause you to abandon the process. Giving birth to an authentic and purposeful life is like all noble creative processes: *The memory of the labor mystically fades as you experience the beauty and joy of the creation.* As you ride the inevitable highs and lows of your wisdom journey, resist the temptation to label any of your experiences along the way as "good" or "bad" based on the emotional charge they carry. Focus instead on what each experience is seeking to teach you, and on understanding more about yourself in the process.

Savor the sweet seasons, too. You'll dance in the lightness of being free from the superficial artifacts of the life you've left behind. You will bask in deep laughter and cherish the purifying warmth of tears. You will intimately know the beauty of ever-expanding divine love in your relationship with the Creator, yourself, and others. You will become even more enlightened about yourself and gain a more pristine clarity about what you are here to offer the world. Joyfully, you will celebrate as the life that you only once imagined continues to take form. As you move forward anchor yourself in a truth that too often goes unacknowledged—one that resides deep within you and is better understood by you than anyone else.

BELIEVE IN YOUR OWN WONDER

Here's something you can bank on: your own wonder. Own it and believe in it. Pause and bless this moment by reflecting upon the power of your journey thus far. Often we expend so much energy being in awe of the external world that we lose touch with the glory and strength residing within us. As a result, our resolve is weakened and we wonder if we really have what it takes to play full-out in the game of life. Something interesting happens when we take inventory of the places we've been, the people we've encountered, and the lessons we've learned along the way. An earnest appreciation for just how miraculous we *already* are rises to the surface of our consciousness. Keeping this awareness close provides the fortitude needed to press onward in your quest for more purposeful living.

Even as a work in progress, you're "soooo amazing" (Luther Vandross voice). Rings true, doesn't it? The fact that you picked up this book seeking greater revelations of the gifts, talents, and abilities within you is proof positive that you are endowed with everything needed to answer Spirit's higher call on your life. Not only do you have what it takes to live a divinely guided and purposeful life, everything you've experienced up until this moment has equipped you to do so. Those who silently witnessed your crucifixions, along with those who contributed nails, now marvel at how beautifully resurrection becomes you. You, my dear sister, are the force of the ocean at high tide. You, beloved, can do all things; and no purpose of yours can be thwarted. Just keep pressing!

LIVING AN INSPIRED LIFE

The folks in your house can tell what kind of day it's going to be when they hear you in the shower belting out your theme song, "I'm Every Woman," before the sun has even stirred. Using that long-handled loofah sponge as your microphone, you spin around and cry out, "Chaka Khan!" three times before the birds have offered their first morning chirps. They're thinking, *Yep, she's going full tilt today!* You're feeling really good. Your entire life has become a celebration of the Divine.

When you are living an inspired life, the breath of Spirit is evident in every area of your life. The attributes of consciousness you've worked to cultivate now show up in your sphere of affairs. The pattern of unsteady turbulence of the past has calmed. Your outer world now reflects more and more of your awakened activity of mind. The inspired life is a beautiful life. You find yourself surrounded with interesting people who are also on a purposeful life journey. All of the love, support, and encouragement you've been giving is being reflected back to you. Your heart sings an eternal course of "Thank you, Divine Presence, for my life."

Serendipity becomes commonplace. The right people show up at the right time offering the right opportunities, insights, and support to help you fulfill your life's mission. Meaningful work that engages your mind and touches your heart is at hand. The loveship you've been seeking arrives and it's everything you'd prayed it would be. You're living a *really* good life! Your desire to help others do the same is stirred. You want people to have what you've got, so you offer yourself to life as an emissary of love. The world is a better place because you are here.

Thank you for allowing me to be a part of your journey. Writing to you and reflecting upon what I was writing you has edified me in wonderful ways. The process of writing this book has supported me in becoming clearer about my own life and the ways that Spirit is seeking greater expression through and as me. I am grateful for your partnership in my continued unfoldment. As you prepare to put down this book and return to the majesty of your life, I offer this parting prayer:

May you experience the ever unfolding
goodness of God
in every area of your life.
May your comings and your goings
be guided and guarded
by the power and presence of the Holy Spirit.
May the rising of each day
and the resting of each night
bring you deeper
into the revelation of Spirit
in, through, and as your life.
I pray for you:
love,
joy,
peace,
health,
and happiness
beyond your wildest imaginings.
And so it is.
Selah.

Acknowledgments

Asante Sana (thank you very much) to all whose work, creativity and support contributed to the completion of this book. I'm grateful for each and every one of you who believed in me and encouraged me to continue writing.

Many passages in this book began as reflections, poems and journal entries. Periodically, I shared bits and pieces with family, friends, colleagues and fellow writers who were also honing their craft. My sincerest appreciation to each of you who took the time to read or listen to my work. Your encouragement and interest in hearing my voice helped me to hold on to the high vision of becoming an author.

To my family: My parents—Caldwell and Electa—thank you for loving me well and giving your all to provide me with the best life possible. My passion for reading and writing, my devotion to Spirit, and commitment to uplifting our people is rooted in your example. To my heart and soul—Kofi—thank you for being such a loving and supportive son. Being your Mom is my greatest joy.

This book wouldn't have been possible without the generosity of the amazing women who shared their personal stories and entrusted me to bring them to life on these pages. Thank you for your openness and honesty. You inspire me—and now many others.

To the editorial team: Thank you for the guidance and feedback that you provided as the manuscript progressed through its various stages of evolution. Ann, Steven, Dawn, Joycelyn, Robin and Janina—your contributions are greatly appreciated.

To the design team: Ian, Alan and Domini—your aesthetic eye and attention to detail resulted in an absolutely stunning cover and interior book design. Thank you for bringing the beautiful.

To Minister Farrakhan: Your lovingkindness has lifted me. Many speak eloquently of love. Some write brilliantly of love. But the greatest teachers of love are those who walk in her light. You—Brother-Minister—are the greatest teacher of love. Thank you for everything.

To my friends who believed in me and offered encouragement. Thank you for having my back and truly being present. It pains me not to list you all, but I tried and then became concerned about missing someone. You know who you are. Know, too, that your love, patience and steadfast support mean the world to me.

Throughout the book I've paid homage to some of the great creative souls whose work has moved and inspired me over the years. These writers, musicians, artists, activists, innovators and thought leaders have blessed me with their genius and I'm forever grateful that they've shared their gifts with the world.

To my readers: Thank you for joining me on this grand adventure. I hope that you've enjoyed the journey and consider it to have been worthwhile. Until we meet again . . .

Every Blessing,
Angela